ESTHER ENERGY

5 Principles for Women of Influence

Written by

Reka Leftridge

Foreword by

Ceceily M. Dowell

Printed in the United States of America

For more information or to book an event, contact:

reka@virtualgoalmind.com

ISBN Paperback: 979-8-9988886-0-1

ISBN Hardcover: 979-8-9988886-1-8

ISBN E-Book: 979-8-9988886-3-2

ISBN Audiobook: 979-8-9988886-2-5

Library of Congress Control Number: 2025913278

DEDICATION

To my amazing husband! God knew exactly what He was doing when He brought you into my life. Long before we ever met, He had already written you into my story and let me just say—He did not disappoint. Thank you for being my calm, my covering, my biggest fan cheering me on. The one who reminds me daily of what unconditional love looks like. The best part of all this is I get to do life with my best friend. Plus, you FINE!

To my incredible kids, you are truly my greatest teachers. Thank you for showing me how to love harder, forgive faster, and laugh from my soul. Being your mom is the greatest honor of my life. You give me purpose, joy, and endless inspiration. This book, this journey, this moment—it's all for you.

FOREWORD

There are books that inform, and then there are books that awaken. This one does both. Esther Energy is for the woman who's been praying for clarity, healing, and truth wondering when the answer would come, not realizing it would arrive wrapped in testimony, drenched in Scripture, and delivered through pages that feel like a divine encounter. It's more than words; it's a sacred invitation. A reminder that God still speaks, still moves, and still calls His daughters to rise. When I first met Reka, it was virtually. A simple introduction turned into a two-hour, spirit-led conversation that neither of us expected but both of us needed. In that moment, what started as a connection quickly became confirmation. We were two women in transition, tired of cycles, hungry for more, and standing at the edge of a life we couldn't quite explain but knew we were being prepared for.

Through that divine exchange, purpose began to rise from the ashes of our surrender, and a sisterhood was born. This book is not just about Queen Esther. It's about the Esther within you. It's not just a study; it's prophetic guidance. A roadmap for the woman who has ever felt overlooked, hidden, silenced, or uncertain about her place in the world. It speaks to the one who has been faithful behind the scenes, showing up for everyone else, but quietly questioning if she's truly called to reign. "Our authority isn't based on what we feel. It's rooted in the promises of Scripture." It's for the woman standing on the edge of her next season. She feels the shift, hears the whisper, but struggles to believe she's worthy to wear the crown. It's for the woman who's not just praying to be seen but praying to be chosen, trusted, and aligned with God's timing.

There's a process before the promise, and often that process includes pruning, pressing, and preparation, and in these pages, you'll find proof that you're not alone. You'll meet a sister who dared to say "yes" when it was hard, who stepped forward when fear said, "stay back," and who let her story become someone else's survival guide. Reka's ability to take her own story and turn it into this book—just for you— is the very essence of the belief that "Faith isn't just about the first step; it's about every step after that. The hard ones. The uncertain ones." Reka has lived this experience fully and because she has, you can, too. She reminds you that your story matters. That your scars are not a sign of shame; they are proof that you in fact did survive what was meant to take you out. You'll see how God uses the very things we thought disqualified us to qualify us for our calling. Maybe, just maybe, you're in a season where God feels silent, and you can't quite hear Him for yourself.

Let this be the reminder to cleave to those who see something in you that you can't yet see. Let their faith stir yours and their fire reignite your own. "What started as brokenness was now a testimony of grace. What felt like abandonment was always His divine orchestration." Through these pages, you will be reminded of your worth, your calling, and your divine positioning. You'll rediscover the grace, discipline, and courage required to walk in royal identity, on purpose, and without apology. I hope you allow Reka's words and her wisdom throughout this book to become another piece of hope and faith, whether you're still in the waiting or stepping boldly into your appointed place, let this book be your mirror, your map, and your sacred reminder.

You are not behind.
You are not forgotten.
You are not too late.
You were born for such a time as this.

Ceceily M. Dowell,

Image & Identity Strategist | Founder, Ceceily Maraya & Company

Contents

ELEVATE

Elevation begins the moment you stop second-guessing your calling and start standing in your God-given authority."

G irl, let me tell you, if you're holding this book right now, it's no accident. I know this may sound clichéd, but you've just taken the first step on a journey that's about to flip the script on your whole life. Not just for inspiration's sake—but so you can fully walk in your *divine assignment* and rise as the woman of influence you were always meant to be. I hope when you read this book, you have the same feeling I had while writing it, and that is, there's no time for Playing small, and Settling season is canceled. It's time to embrace your God-given authority, walk in power, and make the kind of impact you were predestined to make.

You're here because those dreams and goals you've been carrying are big and should be because we serve a big GOD. You've got a vision, and deep down, you know you're not meant to sit on the sidelines of your life. Let me tell you, girl, the first rule of this game? Preparation. We're not just talking about your typical get "organized and make a to-do list" type of prep. Nope, this is about something deeper. It's about stepping into the fullness of who you are, owning your purpose, and recognizing that God didn't put you here by accident.

Before we get too deep, let me introduce myself properly—I'm Reka, your new bestie, and, if not now, by the end of the book, I will be. Beyond that, I'm a Jesus-loving, big-dreaming, purpose-chasing woman. God allowed me to defy the odds and become everything that society deemed I wouldn't. I wear a lot of hats—wife, mother, decorated veteran, visionary, college graduate, mentor, speaker, entrepreneur, encourager, and your cheat-on-coffee-with-tea type of friend. At the heart of it all, I'm a fierce advocate for women, especially mothers living their purpose-driven lives—because, *Baby, we had Purpose before Pampers.* Now, let me take you back for a second and give you a short origin story. You know what they say, and to see where you are going, you must first understand where you came from.

My story began on February 14th, the sweetest day of the year, but trust me, my life was anything but sweet in the beginning. My mother was an addict and alcoholic, and the only thing I knew about my father was his name. I saw things no child should see and lived through moments that hardened me before I even knew what innocence was. While some kids sat around a dinner table eating home-cooked meals, I remember digging through dumpsters for food. While some little girls played with dolls with their moms, I was helping mine up the wrought iron steps after she fell and busted her mouth from drinking too much. And yet—through all the trauma, there were still glimpses of normal.

I can still see my mom walking me to the bus stop, hear the echoes of laughter with my friends during recess, and feel the burning sensations on my hands while learning to cook bacon. Those moments during the day didn't erase the pain, but it was a vast contrast to the night. As a little girl, I grew up in some pretty rough places— liquor houses and pool halls were just a part of my reality. By the time I was nine, I was taken from my mom and placed into foster care. That night felt like something straight out of a Lifetime movie. My mother was screaming, me hiding under the porch, police officers shining bright lights in my face, searching for signs of injury.

My heart pounded as I crouched in the dirt, wishing I could disappear. Then, I was in the back of a police car. Muffled voices up front. Silence. Then a door shut. "Okay, little lady, let's get you somewhere to sleep tonight." And just like that, my life changed. That was the start of me bouncing from foster home to foster home, hoping that it would only be for a few nights. I'd get to go back home to my mother any day now, but days turned into months. Those months were filled with me getting my hand spanked by rulers and fights on the bus because I was the "ugly black girl" until one day, an inkling of hope.

I sat in the judge's chambers—cold, surrounded by towering bookshelves—waiting, hoping, wishing that he'd send me back home with my mom so that this whole nightmare would finally be over. I always wondered what was said in that courtroom. Whatever it was, it wasn't enough because I never went home. The last time I saw my mother was in a bathroom during a meeting my caseworker had arranged. No words were spoken. Not one. I just clung to her legs, terrified of letting go. For a few brief moments, time felt frozen. She didn't say anything; even now, I wonder what she could have said. What words could she have said to make any of this make sense to a little girl whose whole world was slipping away?

Now that I'm a mom myself, I empathize with her. It brings tears to my eyes just thinking about it—I can't imagine having to leave any of my kids. I've spent many days wondering what that did to her mentally, what it felt like to walk away, knowing she couldn't take me with her. After that encounter, I was sent back to a foster home, and it felt like a part of me was gone forever. I officially had nothing to hold onto. That's the day love left.

Both my brother and I were in the system. We had already learned what it felt like to be passed around, shuffled from place to place like pieces on a game board. But my caseworker was diligent. She saw that my brother had my grandmother listed as next of kin and reached out to see if she could take me in, too, but she couldn't. She was too old to care for another child. So, instead, she gave my caseworker my aunt's number.

Thank God for my aunt and uncle, who welcomed me into their home along with their two children. You'd think things got better after that, and, in some ways, they did. But my mind and heart were still stuck in survival mode. I can still picture it—getting off that plane and stepping onto solid ground. My aunt was right there, arms open wide, ready to pull me into an embrace . . . and I just stood there. I don't even think I smiled.

To me, this was just another stop. Another place where I was going to take up space. Deep down, I wondered, *how long would I be here before they sent me back?* Because that's what always happened. I was always sent back. One of the hardest things I struggled with was knowing how to love. Love felt foreign—like something I couldn't wrap my head or arms around. I didn't show affection, and I barely said, "I love you." I didn't feel connected to anyone, even in a house full of people who cared for me.

It took time before I came around, and let me tell you—back then, getting your child therapy wasn't even a thing. If anybody needed therapy, it was your girl right here. Instead, therapy was just going to church, and even that, which was supposed to be a place of comfort, often left me feeling ashamed. The church didn't always feel safe. It felt like a place where you had to stand in front of a congregation and be reminded that everything you had been through somehow was *your* fault. It made it even harder for me to open up and love. Living that kind of life had me terrified to love anyone or anything—because, deep down, I thought it all would be taken away.

So, I built thick walls around my heart. I thought if I could keep people out, I could protect myself from the hurt I was adamant would come. I can still remember how I wasn't used to having free access to food—so I would sneak and hoard it under my bed. My aunt would find it and spank me. I was so numb I wouldn't even cry.

I would just stand there, let the pain pass through me, and then walk away. And *that* made her even angrier. I remember my cousin—who was like a brother—whispering, "Just cry, and it'll be over faster."

I would just shrug my shoulders and keep it moving because I had already learned that tears wouldn't change a thing at that point. By then, I had already cried myself to sleep more nights than I could count. And what had it changed? Nothing. So, I stopped. Stopped crying. Stopped hoping. Stopped expecting anything different because life had already taught me—no matter how many tears I shed, the outcome would stay the same. Even though I was finally living in a home, my mind hadn't caught up to my reality. I was always on guard, always bracing for the worst because that's what life had taught me to expect.

At a young age, I was introduced to the concept of God. When I lived in my longest foster home, the family were Jehovah's Witnesses. They had strict rules and a structured way of doing things, and I learned about God through their lens. Then, when I moved in with my aunt, I found myself in a Pentecostal church, surrounded by fire-filled preaching, shouting, and people being filled with the Holy Spirit.

It was like stepping into a completely different world—polar opposites. But through it all, there was one thing that stuck with me. It wasn't the differences in doctrine, rules, sermons, or traditions; it was prayer because no matter where I went, prayer was always there. At the foster home, I watched them bow their heads and whisper to God. At my aunt's church, I saw people cry out in desperation, hands lifted high.

Two different styles. Same message. God hears. In a world that felt like it was constantly shifting beneath my feet, prayer became the one thing that never changed. It became my lifeline—the only thing no one could take away, my relationship with God. Even when life felt unstable, and I had no control over where I was going next, prayer carried me. I'm sharing this not for a pity party but to show you that your upbringing doesn't define your future or limit the impact that God has called you to make.

Sis, let's be real—we *all* second-guess ourselves sometimes. We question whether we're qualified for what God has called us to do. But here's the truth: the moment you embrace your title as a *Child of God,* it's like unlocking a whole new level of who you are. Seriously, it's like leveling up in a video game! You might not feel like that cool character with all the flashy power moves—and that's okay. Being God's daughter doesn't mean you'll always feel confident or fully prepared. It means you're chosen, equipped, and covered… even when it doesn't feel like it.

It can be unpredictable, even frustrating., but that's part of the journey. Uncovering the real you and tapping into the gifts God planted in you before you even knew they were there. Now listen—there have been moments when I've looked back at my own life and thought, *"I don't even know how I got through that."* Then, add motherhood to the equation. You and I both know how crazy life can get—especially when you're juggling mom life *and* trying to run a business. There are mornings when I wake up with the best intentions, ready to conquer the world. I'm like, *"Okay, I'm gonna get everything done today."*

But before I even finish my coffee? Reality hits. I've already missed my gym alarm. The kiddo can't find her shoes. I'm rushing out the door and already late for drop-off. My inbox is giving side-eye because emails are stacking up like laundry. And right when I think I have a second to breathe, here comes the dreaded question—*"Mom, what's for dinner?"* And just like that… the day spirals before it even begins. Sound familiar?

We're out here juggling everything—business meetings while answering school emails. School pickups while mentally drafting a to-do list. Cooking dinner while folding laundry. Trying to remember if we even drank water today. We are the chef, the Uber, the chaos coordinator, the problem solver, and yes—sometimes we drop the ball. The permission slip doesn't get signed. The laundry sits in the dryer (for the third day in a row). The business idea we were excited about is still sitting in the notes app. And if we're not careful, guilt creeps in—whispering that we should be doing more.

Let me pause here and remind you of something, sis: there's *no* room for guilt where grace lives. We were never called to be perfect.

The real power is not in checking every box or doing everything right. It's in knowing that God's grace and mercy are covering us in *every single space* we step into—whether we're managing our homes, building our businesses, or just trying to make it through the day without losing it.

Sometimes, life feels like a video game. You're running hard, dodging obstacles, trying to level up—and just when you think you've got the rhythm down... *BOOM!* You hit a wall. That's when hustle isn't enough. That's when you need help. You need *Power-Ups*.

Remember Super Mario Bros.? (Yep, I'm taking you way back.) Mario's out there sprinting through fire pits and jumping over Goombahs, trying to take him out. But he's not just running aimlessly—he's grabbing Power-Ups. Not just to get bigger but to go faster, jump higher, and win the level.

That's exactly how God's grace and mercy work in our lives.

Grace is getting something good when you don't deserve it— strength when you feel weak, favor when you've fallen short, peace when everything around you is chaotic.

Mercy is when God holds back judgment or punishment and instead shows compassion, reminding you that you're still loved and worthy.

Grace lifts you, and mercy covers you. Together, they remind you that God isn't waiting for you to be perfect—He's offering help for the journey. So, the next time life throws something your way that knocks the wind out of you, don't give up. You've got access to supernatural Power Ups that shows us that God's love isn't based on performance, its freely given. You just have to tap in.

I get it, sis—it's scary. Even as I sit here writing this, the uncertainty creeps in. *Who's going to buy this book? Is anyone even going to read it? What if this was all a waste of time?* I wish I could tell you I don't have these thoughts. But I do. And if we're being real? You do, too. That little voice that whispers, "You're not good enough. You're not qualified. Nobody's checking for you." But whenever those thoughts start getting loud, I go straight to the cheat codes—Scripture.

One of my favorites reminds us, "For God has not given us a spirit of fear, but of power and of love and of a sound mind" (2 Timothy 1:7). Because fear will have you shrinking, questioning every move, doubting what God already spoke over you. Whenever we start playing small, God's Word reminds us of who we truly are and the power we already possess. When we root ourselves in Scripture, we tap into a strength that doesn't come from us but *through* us. That's where real courage lives. It gives us the muscle to push towards our calling, even when we feel completely unqualified. I've always loved the saying, *"God doesn't call the qualified; He qualifies the called."* Whew— *that's* been my truth. And if you're being honest with yourself? Sis, it's probably yours too.

The other day, I saw an Instagram post asking, "If you could ask any woman in the Bible a question, who would it be?" Without a doubt, for me, that woman would be Esther. Talk about the ultimate example of a woman who refused to play small—Queen Esther. I can't help but wonder what it must have felt like to realize that her position wasn't just about her. That her purpose was tied to an entire nation's deliverance. Now that's an impact. If you're unfamiliar with her story, let me tell you—girlfriend had it going on. Forgive my '90s slang, but your girl was "bomb dignity, no doubt. "But let's be clear— she didn't just wake up one day and save her people.

Esther was never supposed to be queen… at least not by the world's standards. She wasn't born into royalty. She was a Jewish orphan named Hadassah, raised by her cousin Mordecai after the death of her parents. There was nothing about her upbringing that screamed "divine destiny." She was quiet, unseen, and unlikely, but the unlikely are God's specialty.

The book of Esther stands out in the Bible because it doesn't mention God by name—not once. No "YHWH." No "Elohim." Yet, His fingerprints are all over the story. While His name isn't written, His presence is undeniable. God was there—guiding, orchestrating, and positioning Esther in a place of influence, all without announcing Himself. Esther wasn't just selected for the palace; she was positioned for purpose.

At first, she tried to blend in. She even changed her name from Hadassah to Esther. Maybe it felt safer to hide her true identity. Perhaps she believed she could just exist quietly in the background. But sis, when you're chosen, hiding isn't an option for long. God has a funny way of keeping you hidden until it's time to use you. And when He calls you? There's no staying in the background.

Esther went from an unknown orphan girl to a queen whose name will forever be synonymous with obedience and humility. Before she ever wore a crown or stepped foot in the palace, Esther was hidden—in God. He worked on her secretly, developing her character in silence, molding her strength in quiet places. While the world couldn't see it, God prepared her for a purpose far greater than her position. And here's something powerful you may not have known: the Hebrew root of Esther's name is Hester, meaning *"hidden."* That hidden season? It wasn't punishment. It was *preparation.*

Esther was beautiful on the outside, yes, but it was her *inner beauty* that carried the real weight. Her grace, humility, faith, and obedience made her royal long before the crown ever touched her head. Even as queen, she didn't lose her closeness with God. She didn't forget where her strength came from. That intimacy with Him gave her the courage to walk in boldness and fulfill the assignment placed on her life.

So, sis, if you're in a season where you feel unseen or overlooked—*don't resent it.* You're not hidden because you're unworthy. You're hidden because you're *being refined.* God is shaping you in the secret place. When you start second-guessing whether God really has a specific purpose for *you*, pause and remember this: *"You were born for such a time as this." — Esther 4:14*

Preparation isn't just about setting a few goals and checking boxes. Real preparation is a heart posture and a mindset shift. It's knowing that your journey is *always* evolving—just like your purpose, your business, and your faith walk. It's about sharpening your skills, deepening your trust in God, and building the kind of resilience that can't be shaken by circumstances. Because, girl, the way you *think* determines how you *show up*. Before Esther stepped into royalty—she underwent an *intense* season of preparation.

Scripture tells us she went through twelve months of beauty treatments—*six months with oil of myrrh and six with perfumes and cosmetics* (Esther 2:12). That's a full year of refining, softening, and sanctifying—on the outside *and* the inside. Talk about consecration, she was truly set apart. Now, let's break that down because it wasn't just a spa day or luxury self-care. This was sacred.

The oil of myrrh wasn't just for fragrance—it was used for *purification and healing*. Myrrh represents the pressing, surrender, and letting go. It's bitter yet beautiful. It signifies the death of the old so the new can emerge. For six months, Esther had to soak in that oil. That meant time, stillness, and allowing the old layers to be stripped away so she could become who God called her to be.

Then came six months with perfumes and cosmetics—the part that beautified her outwardly, yes, but also signified *favor, presentation, and readiness*. It was about being *positioned* to walk confidently in front of royalty. She went through a process to walk confidently into purpose: to move with wisdom, carry herself with grace, and walk in rooms she once could not have imagined herself in.

So, if it feels like you're in the middle of a stretch—emotionally, mentally, spiritually—it's not in vain. You're not stuck; you're *being shaped*. You can't skip the oil and get to the crown. God is more concerned with your *becoming* than your arriving. So let Him do the work.

Let the oil heal. Let the fragrance rise. Because when your moment comes—and it *will* —you won't just look the part. You'll *be* the woman who's been prepared for the palace.

Esther's story is more than a historical account—it's a powerful testament to *divine appointment*. As a woman of influence, her journey reminds us that where we are—whether in life, careers, or ministry—isn't random. It's not luck or a coincidence. It's *calling*. Your role, your voice, your platform?

It is all by *design.*

Esther didn't chase visibility. She answered a divine summons. When the moment came, she didn't let fear silence her purpose. She stood in bold obedience, and in doing so, she saved a nation. That's not just Bible history—that's a blueprint.

While your path may not look exactly like Esther's, the principles she lived by—obedience, courage, humility, and divine timing—are universal.

So, as we dive deeper into this chapter, remember this: None of your dreams, influence, or business is by chance. It's all part of a divine design, and now is the time to step into that place with full confidence, ready to own your power like the queen you are. You've got purpose, passion, and endless possibility on your side —and trust me, sis, with God in your corner, you're unstoppable.

A Call to Step Out in Faith

Now let me share a moment that flipped my world upside down— a moment that forced me to step out in faith, just like Esther. My husband and I were serving in the military, and it was time for me to return to sea duty—meaning I'd be on a ship full-time. Around the same time, the Army wanted to send my husband to an Army base about three hours away for an operational role.

On paper, it sounded like duty as usual. But in reality? It meant both of us would be gone—away from our kids. In the military, we've got something called a Family Care Plan. Basically, you assign guardianship—power of attorney and all—to someone who'll care for your kids when duty calls. But let me tell you, that plan sat heavy on our hearts. Every conversation ended with me saying, "I'm not sending my kids anywhere." And I meant it.

At the time, we had three kids at home, two in high school and one in elementary. One morning, I was sitting in the gym, earbuds in, but completely lost in thought. Right there, in that quiet space with the weights clanking in the background and my heart racing from more than just the workout, I felt an undeniable pull from within. It was like God was whispering, "Choose your peace. Choose your purpose. Trust Me." After many late-night talks with my husband—and even more talks with God—I made a decision that felt like I was stepping off a cliff. I put in my retirement papers. This should have felt easy, but it wasn't.

At the time, I was the top Navy Chief Petty Officer at my duty station. I was eligible for advancement, and I dreamed of becoming Senior Chief to be real with you. Actually? Master Chief. I had worked hard for this advancement. Yet, I knew this next move was about more than rank; it was about obedience. It was about putting my family first in a way that honored who I was becoming. It was about trusting God with the version of me I hadn't seen yet. The Army held up its end, and my husband was assigned to a duty station in Killeen—three hours away. Since our oldest was just one year away from graduating from high school, we both knew uprooting the kids just wasn't an option.

So, we made a decision that would quietly shape the next few years of our lives—I stayed in San Antonio with the kids. My husband moved alone. For the next four years, he was only home on the weekends. Sis, let me tell you—that kind of separation wears on you. When I thought I had adjusted and had a rhythm and routine going, life hit me with another curveball. I found out I was pregnant with our fourth child. Yep. Plot twist. And as if that wasn't enough, the world shut down—COVID-19 hit. Pregnancy in a pandemic? That was a new level of stress I hadn't even imagined. I managed three kids at home—all virtual learners—trying to figure out schedules, screens, snacks, and sanity.

All while hiding my first trimester symptoms because the last time, we'd lost the baby, and I didn't want to explain the loss to the kids again. The fear of another miscarriage? It stayed with me. Quiet, heavy, constant. I didn't want to speak it, but I felt it. So, I tried to keep it together for the kids, the house, and myself. But girl . . . Hiding morning sickness while pretending to be "just fine" in the kitchen? Sneaking off to vomit in the bathroom while helping with math homework five minutes later? That's a kind of strength they don't write enough about.

There were days I felt like I was drowning. Not just busy—but bone-deep tired. I couldn't come up for air; it felt like everything was pressing down on me. There were mornings I didn't want to get out of bed. Days where I felt buried beneath duty and sacrifice. Whether I made the right decision lay beneath all of the stress. But in those dark moments, I did the only thing I knew how to do —I leaned into my faith. I reminded myself, you didn't walk away from the military on a whim. You stepped away because you believed God had something greater for you and your family. Even though I couldn't see the whole picture, I held onto that truth like a lifeline.

Just like Esther, I knew my journey wasn't just about me. There was a bigger purpose behind all of this—even if I couldn't see it yet. So, I prayed. I prayed for strength when I felt like I had none left. I prayed for guidance when I didn't know what to do. I prayed for peace when the chaos of life felt louder than God's voice. Can I be honest with you? There were days after my husband left, I would sit by the door, tears streaming down my face before I could even try to stop them, knowing we had three more years of living separately. I was determined to be everything for the kids while feeling like a part of me was missing.

Keeping it all together for them was the hardest part. I didn't want them to see me break because I didn't want them to break too! But God! We've all had those moments where it feels like life is pressing in from all sides—when you wonder if you'll ever make it to the other side. But somehow—by His grace, we do. When I retired, this was not the life I had pictured. If I'm being honest? Your girl thought she was about to live the dream. I had visions of traveling the world, sipping lattes in cute cafés in different time zones, spending my days wrapped in white robes at five-star spas with eucalyptus steam and deep-tissue massages on rotation. And don't even start with how I knew I was about to be that Instagram gym girlie—You know, the one. Matching gym sets. Flawless morning routine. Skin glowing. Protein smoothie in hand. What did I get instead? A front-row seat to growth, stretching, and divine realignment.

While the dream looked one way—God had something more purposeful in mind. But reality? Reality hit differently. I didn't expect it to be this hard. The transition. The uncertainty. The weight of it all. But if there was one thing I knew for sure—I had to set the tone for my home, no matter how I felt on the inside. So, as much as I wanted to crawl under the covers and wait for life to make sense, I woke up each day and continued to show up—not because it was easy, but because I understood that what I was carrying was bigger than myself. Stepping out in faith wasn't just a moment; it became a journey. Those surrendered moments when I whispered, *"God, I trust You,"* taught me something faith-shifting.

Faith isn't just about having the courage to take the first step — it's about trusting God enough to take *every step after it*, especially when the path isn't clear. There were times I couldn't see the full picture. Times when I questioned if I was even on the right track. But in those moments, I remembered something powerful: I may not see the masterpiece, but I *know* the Artist. Each step— even the hard,

14

uncomfortable ones—was a stroke on the canvas of my purpose. God was guiding me, even when I felt unsure. Emotions are meant to be *felt*, not followed. They're indicators—not instructors. Just like Esther, I was being *positioned* for something greater. And I couldn't let my *emotions* lead the way.

It's easy to get caught up in our feelings and let our circumstances shape our self-image, making us vulnerable to the lies about our identity whispered by our struggles. But here's the truth: our circumstances do not define us. Not the chaos, the betrayal, or the valley you're navigating right now. God didn't just call you—He equipped you. That's why, even when the pressure, exhaustion, and fear feel overwhelming; you can still walk confidently in your God-given authority. This power doesn't come from ease or understanding everything that happens but because you know who you are and whose you are. You can still stand in that truth even when you feel like your legs are about to give out.

Walking in Your God-Given Authority

Sis, let's talk about real power—not the kind that shows up when everything's going right but stands firm when everything feels like it's falling apart. Our authority doesn't come from how we feel on any given day. It's not based on how confident we sound or how flawless our planner looks. No, our authority is rooted in something far more unshakable—what *God* said. John 10:10 doesn't just whisper—it declares: Jesus came so we could have life. And not just any life. A life filled with abundance.

Now, when we hear "abundance," our minds go straight to money, and success. But God's version of abundance? It's deeper. Fuller. Richer. He's talking about a life overflowing with peace when everything's chaotic. Joy when the world feels cold. And that sweet purpose—even when the path feels confusing. There were days when I didn't feel strong. When I couldn't hold it all together. When the tears came without warning. And maybe you've had those days, too.

But Romans 8:28 reminds us that none of it is wasted—not the heartache, the confusion, or the waiting seasons. God is working *all* of it together for our good because we're called according to *His* purpose.

And when you're too tired to be strong 2 Corinthians 12:9 is like a hug from heaven: *"My grace is sufficient for you, for My power is made perfect in weakness."* That means you don't have to fake it or carry it all. His grace fills the gaps. True power begins with recognizing your authority in Christ—when you understand who you are in Him, everything around you starts to shift. Rooms change. Atmospheres respond.

Walking in your God-given authority can feel intimidating, especially when the world wants you to doubt your worth. But here's the truth: this authority didn't originate with you, and it's not dependent on how "ready" you feel. Jesus Himself gave it to us. Through His death and resurrection, He didn't just save us—He empowered us. Luke 10:19 says, *"I have given you authority... over all the power of the enemy."* That's not a gentle encouragement—it's a divine commissioning.

You've been handed absolute, spiritual authority, and now it's your responsibility to stand in it, speak from it, and move with it—because the Kingdom moves when you do.

Recognizing Your Authority

Now let's be real—when Esther became queen, she probably had a moment of, Wait . . . who me? Who am I to handle this? Am I built for this level of responsibility? And, if we are being honest, haven't we all had similar moments? However, as her story unfolds, we witness her go from who am I to why not me. She confidently embraces her authority and begins to act with clarity and conviction.

That transformation didn't happen overnight. It took time for Esther to realize that her authority wasn't rooted in her strength; it came from God. I know those feelings of inadequacy can creep in like uninvited guests. Imposter syndrome. Self-doubt. Fear. All trying to whisper, "Girl, please! You are not cut out for this." But, sis, let me remind you—just like Esther, you've been chosen and equipped. Your authority doesn't come from perfection. It comes from the One who called you. God has already given you everything you need—

The gifts.
The talents.
The experiences.
The voice.

You are not leading alone. In every role you carry—mother, wife, business leader, or influencer—you are partnering with God. That truth should bring peace to your spirit, confidence to your steps, and a deep sigh of relief. You don't have to have all the answers. God does. Let that sink in: You are already walking in power. You are influenced—but not by the noise of the world. You are influenced by the steps God has predestined for you.

Women of Influence: Who They Are, How to Identify If You Are One, and How to Become One

Some women have the ability to enter a room and change the atmosphere. It's not just their presence; it's what they exemplify. They are grounded in something deeper than charisma or confidence—they embody influence. According to the Oxford English Dictionary, Influence is defined as the capacity to affect the character, development, or behavior of someone or something, or the effect itself. This type of influence does not come from titles, platforms, or applause; it arises from confidently embracing who God created you to be. A woman of influence leads with purpose, speaks with intention, acts with integrity, and supports others as she rises. The truth is, that woman isn't "out there"—she is already within you. All you need to do is start walking in that truth.

How to Identify If You Are a Woman of Influence

Sis, if you've ever wondered, *Am I really a woman of influence?* let me ask you this:

- ☞ Do people look to you for guidance, wisdom, or encouragement?
- ☞ Have you ever inspired someone to step out in faith or overcome their fears?
- ☞ Do you feel a deep calling to serve, lead, or create a meaningful impact in some way?
- ☞ Are you willing to grow, learn, and embrace what God has in store for you?

How to Become a Woman of Influence

If you want to step fully into your influence, it starts with these three things:

Know Who You Are in Christ

A woman of influence is grounded in her identity, not in insecurity. She does not seek validation from others because she knows to whom she belongs. To lead effectively, you must first be led —by God, by wisdom, and by purpose.

Develop a Heart for Service

Influence isn't about status; it's about serving others. Impactful leaders don't strive for power; they aim to empower those around them. Whether in motherhood, ministry, or business, your influence is most powerful when it uplifts others.

Lead with Esther Energy

Queen Esther embodied what it means to be a woman of influence—not because of her title, but because of her obedience, wisdom, and courage. This book is your pathway if you're ready to step fully into your influence, impact, and purpose.

What You Can Expect from This Book

This isn't just a book—each chapter is inspired by a letter from Esther's name, breaking down the powerful lessons from her journey and showing you how to apply them to your own life. Through these pages, you'll learn to be driven by faith and empowered by grace—no longer holding back but walking boldly in the authority that God has already given you.

Here's what we'll explore together:

- ☞ **Embracing Your God-Given Authority**: Owning your identity and walking confidently, just like Esther did.

- ☞ **Strategic Preparation** – Learning how to position yourself wisely for the purpose God has for you.

- ☞ **Trusting God Through Transition Seasons**: Waiting doesn't mean being wasted; God is always working behind the scenes.

- ☞ **Humility in Leading** – Understanding that impactful leadership is rooted in servanthood and wisdom.

- ☞ **Endure & Refine in the Off-Season** – The silent seasons are where your strength is built. This isn't just about reading; it's about transformation.

That's why at the end of each chapter, you will find one of the following:

- **Scripture Reflections:** Dive deeper into God's Word and see how it applies to your journey.
- **Prayers:** Because let's be real—you're going to need God's strength to navigate this journey.
- **Declarations:** Speak life over yourself and step into your authority with confidence.
- **Journal Prompts & Reflection Questions:** These will help you process, apply, and grow from what you're learning Throughout the book, you will discover frameworks—a step-by-step guide designed to help you overcome doubt, fear, and hesitation so you can fully embrace the woman God has called you to be.

This book is for the woman who knows there's more—more purpose, more impact, more faith, more confidence—but who just needs a clear path forward. If that resonates with you, then let's get started, sis!

Grab your journal because here are your first Power Action Journal Prompts, along with prayers and scriptures to meditate on.

Journal Prompts

Recognize Your Divine Appointment

What moments in your life clearly demonstrate God's guidance leading you to where you are today?

Reflect on the patterns, divine connections, and open doors that you believe only God could have orchestrated.

Seek Guidance

Are you facing a business or life decision right now?

Spend some quiet time asking God for direction and then journal what you hear or feel led to do.

Finding Strength in Your Voice

Where in your life or business have you remained silent when God called you to speak up? What's one area this week where you can use your voice with fearlessness?

Prayer to Embrace Your Authority

Father God,

Thank You for choosing me, calling me, and equipping me. I am grateful for every closed door, every divine delay, and every moment You've redirected my steps, as I now see that You were preparing me for such a time as this. I surrender my doubts, my fears, and every lie that tells me I'm not enough. I am in constant need of Your guidance. Help me to walk boldly in Your authority. Remind me that it's not about being perfect; it's about being obedient. Lord, move in every part of my life so that it may glorify You. I align my intentions with Your will and ask that You continue to sharpen my discernment, strengthen my faith, and expand my territory.

Let me be a light in every room I enter. Let my work reflect Your glory. And let my legacy point back to You.

In Jesus' name,

Amen

Scriptures for Meditation

1. Esther 4:14 (NIV): *"For if you remain silent at this time, relief and deliverance for the Jews will arise from another place, but you and your father's family will perish. And who knows but that you have come to your royal position for such a time as this?"*

2. Jeremiah 29:11 (NIV): *"'For I know the plans I have for you,' declares the Lord, 'plans to prosper you and not to harm you, plans to give you hope and a future.'"*

3. Romans 8:28 (NIV): *"And we know that in all things God works for the good of those who love him, who have been called according to his purpose."*

4. 4. Proverbs 3:5-6 (NIV): *"Trust in the Lord with all your heart and lean not on your own understanding; in all your ways submit to him, and he will make your paths straight."*

5. Philippians 4:13 (NIV): *"I can do all this through him who gives me strength."*

STRATEGIC
PREPARATION

"Preparation is not just a season—it's a mindset. If you stay ready, you don't have to get ready."

- T. D. Jakes

In the book of Esther, we observe a powerful example of strategic planning. Esther's journey evolves from being a passive participant to an active advocate for her people. This transformation is marked by preparation, wise counsel, patience, discernment, and obedience. She didn't rush into decisions; instead, she sought guidance, assessed the situation, and devised a plan to save her people. Esther's strategic approach provides valuable lessons on preparing, developing, and executing strategies that align with your calling.

If you're anything like me, you've had those moments where you're staring in the mirror, saying to yourself, "There has to be more." That feeling when what you're dreaming of doesn't even come close to your current reality. I've been there—feeling isolated, like everything I was holding onto—even my own identity—was being stripped away. It had me questioning, who am I? What's my purpose? Where do I go from here?

These are what I like to call the wilderness seasons, and they will have you questioning everything. One day, you think you've got it all figured out. You're making boss moves, following the plan you've prayed over, feeling like you know where you're headed. And then, out of nowhere... everything shifts. Suddenly, nothing looks the way you expected. It's like you're walking blind and trying to understand it all, searching for answers that never seem to come fast enough.

Oh, don't get me started on that divine preparation we always hear about—as if it's the simplest thing to embrace. If we're being honest there are moments when it doesn't feel like preparation at all; it feels more like punishment. It's as if every part of your being is stripped of everything, including your identity. The plans you thought would work? Falling apart. The certainty you once had? Gone. And that's when the doubts start creeping in—*Did I make the wrong choice? Did I take a wrong turn? Is this really the path I'm supposed to be on?*

The sense of God's presence that once felt so near seems to have faded, leaving you feeling lost and confused. But, girl, hear me loud and clear—God has not left you. In the grand scheme of things, it's God's way of drawing you closer to Him. He's not just meeting your needs at the moment—He's positioning, molding, refining, and shaping you into the person He's destined you to become.

So often, we cling to a title, a job, or a position, thinking, this is it. I've made it. We become complacent and comfortable. But just when you think you've arrived, God calls you to keep moving forward. The roles you step into are not the end—they are steppingstones, guiding you to the place He's specifically designed for you, with the people He's assigned to you and for you. We've all found ourselves in situations where we felt unprepared, unqualified, overwhelmed, or simply unworthy. That's exactly where God shows up. That's where He shapes you for the next level. The real challenge isn't always the next level—it's what we *think* the next level should look like.

We get stuck in the feelings.
In overthinking.
In the comparison trap.

We start to doubt if we're good enough, ready enough, or worthy enough. But sometimes the next level doesn't come looking like a spotlight—it shows up looking like surrender. And if we're not careful, we'll miss it because we're too busy trying to match someone else's version of success.

One evening, my daughter came in to say goodnight, a moment I still cherish, even now that my kids are older. I was lying in bed reading on my phone when she said, "Oh, Mom, you look like a real mom now!" I was taken aback and asked, "What do you mean?" She pointed out my pajamas, scarf, and glasses, saying I looked like a "real mama." It felt like she was trying to take a dig at me (insert side eye), but it made me think. Isn't that how many of us feel? You might have the experience, titles, and a well-established resume, but the vision God has given you doesn't seem to match your current reality.

But sis—just because you don't *feel* like you look the part, or the whole picture hasn't come together yet, doesn't mean you're not already walking in it. I've learned this firsthand. Raising four kids while on active duty taught me that I was a mama through and through—even when I didn't *look* or *feel* like one. It reminds me of this truth: *"Greater is He who is in you than he who is in the world."* (1 John 4:4)

Your strength was never meant to come from the outside. It comes from the Spirit of God who lives in you. When I finally understood my purpose and embraced my calling, something shifted. I stopped searching for approval. I no longer needed applause to feel qualified. I realized I wasn't created to *perform*—I was called to *walk boldly* in what God had already placed inside of me. That desire to *look* the part is a trap. It will have you trying to look at like the part without *being* the part, leaving you striving, empty, and disconnected from your true identity.

True purpose doesn't require permission or validation. It requires obedience and trust. You don't need to prove you're enough when you're already *chosen*. The world may look for a polished image—but God is building a powerful vessel. When we stop chasing the illusion perfection that's where the power of purpose-driven preparation comes in. For a mom who's running a business or working for one, it's not just about hustling— it's about making sure every action in your life aligns with your purpose-driven Mission.

Understanding your Mission, Vision, and Personal Purpose (MVP) is the key to fulfillment and decisiveness. When you align your actions with your MVP, you're not just making moves in your business or career. You're also reflecting on who you are and what you stand for without sacrificing your family or yourself. This is not just work; it's a purposeful journey, building something impactful and meaningful ordained by God for His glory. It's a partnership with God to bring a vision to pass that He designed specifically for you. That's love. He knows us through and through and still wants to use us.

Before you doubt yourself again, remember this: God uses it all—for His glory, not our own. Every detour, every delay, even your doubts—none of it is wasted in God's hands. But if we're going to walk boldly in our assignment, we need clarity. So before we go deeper, let's talk about establishing your MVP—your Mission, Vision, and Purpose.

Your Mission is your compass. It guides your decisions and helps you navigate the complex intersections of motherhood, career, and calling. It keeps you anchored so you're not swayed by distractions, shiny-object opportunities, or short-term wins that don't align with your long-term vision. I've lived this. There were seasons where I was doing *good* things—successful, impressive things—but deep down, I was craving to do a *God* thing. I didn't just want to be in position—I wanted to be in alignment.

Being in position without being anointed and appointed will leave you feeling powerless. And when you feel powerless, you start to question your worth. You get caught in cycles you were meant to break. That's what a lack of clarity around your MVP looks like.

It shows up as:

- Chronic irritability
- Saying yes to everything
- Feeling unfulfilled
- No boundaries
- Burnout disguised as "being productive"

You stay busy just to *stay busy*—but there's no real purpose or progress to show for it. That's exactly why this 6-step MVP process matters.

It's not just about writing down goals—it's about gaining clarity, building boundaries, and executing what God has *already* placed inside of you. Stepping into your divine assignment doesn't happen by accident—it requires intentionality, preparation, and alignment.

The Power of the 6-Step MVP Process

This process walks you through:

1. **Mission** – Your *Why*
2. **Vision** – Your *Where*
3. **Purpose** – Which includes:
   - **Personal Goals** – Your *How*
   - **Core Values** – Your standards, your guardrails

Think of it as your Kingdom Roadmap. It grounds you when life feels chaotic and keeps you focused when everything else tries to pull you off course.

Look at Queen Esther. She didn't just walk into the palace and rescue her people overnight. She paused, prayed, and prepared—mentally, spiritually, and strategically. She aligned herself with God's plan before she made her move. The same applies to you. When things feel heavy, this framework will remind you of Who you are, Why you're here, and what truly matters. When you align your mission with God's direction, you don't just work harder—you work *wiser*. You move with authority and steward your calling with confidence, not confusion.

When you know who you are and what you're called to do—it changes how you operate personally and professionally.

Step 1: Define Your Mission (Your "Why")

Your Mission is your God-given assignment—essentially your purpose in this season. It should be specific, personal, and service driven, reflecting on how you are called to impact others. Remember that your purpose isn't just about your gifts; it's about how you use those gifts to serve others, with God at the center. As you grow, your assignment may also evolve.

> **Biblical Foundation:** *"Commit to the Lord whatever you do, and He will establish your plans"* (Proverbs 16:3)

Examples of Personal Mission Statements:

- "I am dedicated to empowering women to embrace their God-given authority by providing them with the tools, strategies, and faith-based principles they need to live courageously and fulfill their purpose."

- "I help moms and entrepreneurs walk in alignment with their faith and business without sacrificing their peace, family, or self-worth."

- "I am committed to utilizing my speaking, writing, and coaching skills to empower women to reclaim their confidence and step into the leadership roles God intended for them."

- "I am committed to creating a loving and nurturing home that honors God, where my family can thrive. My goal is to nurture both my family and my dreams with grace and purpose."

Reflection Questions:

1. What am I deeply passionate about?
2. How has my life experience prepared me for my purpose?
3. Who am I called to serve, and how can I make an impact?

Step 2: Define Your Vision (Your "Where")

Your vision is the bigger picture, where God is leading you. It represents the impact and legacy you want to leave. Your vision is expansive and should excite you while also stretching you beyond your comfort zone.

> **Biblical Foundation:** *"For I know the plans (thoughts) I have for you, declares the Lord, plans to pros-per you and not to harm you, plans to give you hope and a future"* (Jeremiah 29:11).

Examples of Personal Vision Statements:

- "I envision a world where women of faith confidently lead in business, unapologetically walking in their God-given power."

- "My vision is to see a generation of purpose-driven mothers who build wealth, grow in faith, and create a legacy that honors God."

- "I see myself traveling the world, speaking life into women, and creating resources that help them live boldly, courageously, and on purpose."

Reflection Questions:

1. What does success look like for me in alignment with God's purpose?

2. What would that look like if I fully stepped into my calling without fear?

3. What legacy do I want to leave for my family, business, or community?

4. What boundaries do I need to set in order to protect my purpose, time, and energy?

Step 3: Define Your Personal Goals (Your "How")

Your goals are the practical steps you will take to live out your mission and fulfill your vision. These should be specific, measurable, and faith-filled.

Biblical Foundation: *"The plans of the diligent lead to profit as surely as haste leads to poverty"* (Proverbs 21:5).

Example of Personal Goals:

- "Dedicate 30 minutes each morning for prayer, journaling, and strategy planning."

- "Launch a faith-based coaching program to mentor women entrepreneurs."

- "Write and publish my first book on purpose-driven leadership by writing 300 words daily."

- "Create a schedule that prioritizes God, family time while growing my business."

Reflection Questions:

1. What specific steps can I take to fulfill my mission and vision?
2. What skills do I need to develop or improve?
3. What systems do I need to put in place to achieve these goals?

Step 4: Align with Your Core Values (Your "Standards")

Your core values are the principles that keep you grounded. These are non-negotiable standards that guide your decision-making in life, career, or business.

> **Biblical Foundation:** *"But just as He who called you is holy, so be holy in all you do"* (1 Peter 1:15).

Examples of Core Values:

- **Faith:** Keeping God at the center of everything I do
- **Integrity**: Operating in honesty and excellence in business and life
- **Balance.** Prioritizing my faith, family, and business without burnout
- **Growth:** Always learning, evolving, and stepping into new levels
- **Service:** Helping others through wisdom, mentorship, and generosity

Reflection Questions:

1. What principles do I refuse to comprise on?
2. What causes or missions do I feel deeply connected to and want to support?
3. What does success look like to me, and how do I measure it?

Step 5: Write Your Full MVP Declaration

Now that you've defined your Mission, Vision, Personal Goals, and Core Values, let's put it all together into your MVP Declaration.

> **Biblical Foundation:** *"Write the vision and make it plain"* (Habakkuk 2:2).

An example of my MVP Declaration:

"My mission is to empower women to embrace their God-given authority by providing faith-based strategies for both business and personal growth. I envision creating a movement of faith-driven leaders who operate with confidence, clarity, and purpose. My goals include launching a mentorship program, publishing a book, and establishing a sustainable work-life balance that prioritizes both my faith and my family. I am committed to living with integrity, faith, and a spirit of service, understanding that I was called to this purpose for such a time as this."

Step 6: Pray Over Your MVP Statement:

Father God,

Thank You for the purpose You have placed inside me. I surrender my plans, my goals, and my vision to You. Align my steps with Your will and let everything I do reflect Your glory. When doubt tries to creep in, remind me that You have called me for a such a time like this. Equip me with the discipline, focus, and wisdom to walk courageously in my purpose. Let my life be a testimony of Your faithfulness and unfailing love.

In Jesus' name,

Amen.

Please take the time to create your own MVP declaration. Having a Mission, Vision, Personal Goals, and Core Values are key because they help you set boundaries, guide your decision-making, and help you push through challenges with confidence. Remember, we're walking in Queen Energy—just like Esther. She knew her assignment and showed up with grace, boldness, and humility. She stayed rooted in her purpose and values, allowing her to lead and make bold moves. With your own MVP declaration, be sure to make sure that it is grounded in scripture. Remember, "God's word never comes back void" (Isaiah 55:11).

Your MVP declaration isn't just a personal mission statement — it's your spiritual anchor. It empowers you to move with purpose, confidence, and conviction, no matter what comes your way. Look at Esther, she was intentional in her preparation. She didn't just jump into action—she took time to fast, pray, and seek divine guidance. Every step she made was strategic and perfectly aligned with her mission to save her people.

When Mordecai told her about Haman's plan to destroy the Jews, Esther didn't panic, nor did she react out of fear or ego. Instead, she paused and considered the weight of her next move. Initially, she hesitated; but Esther didn't let fear take her out of position. She leaned into the discomfort and chose obedience over ease. Esther understood that her next move could mean life or death, so she devised a strategic plan to approach the king rather than rushing in. Side note: She must have been *"that girl"* because, babe, King Xerxes offered Esther anything she wanted (twice)—even half of his kingdom—and yet, she didn't rush into it.

Let's put this in perspective: the Persian Empire was the wealthiest of its time, valued at over 1 trillion dollars in today's market. Esther wasn't about to make a move without carefully thinking it through. She went to God first. And that's another lesson we can learn from Esther. We can't get so caught up in chasing results that we forget to pause and consult God. When we let Him lead, we move not

33

just with clarity—but with covering. So, stay postured in obedience because when you seek God first, everything else falls into place—just like it did for Esther.

As women with families, careers, and businesses, it's easy to get caught up in the "it has to get done now" mindset. We're constantly multitasking, trying every productivity hack available to avoid burnout. However, the one key factor holding us back, even when pursuing our purpose, is a lack of preparation. Being gifted doesn't exempt us from the necessary prep work. I'll admit that I've been guilty of thinking that just because I was gifted in an area that I could only rely on God's favor at the moment. But oh, girl, the Holy Spirit has a way of humbling you real quick when you start to slack off. God's grace is sufficient, but if we're not preparing for what we are praying for, we risk missing out on opportunities because we aren't mentally, spiritually, or physically ready. If we can't manage what's in front of us, we certainly won't be able to handle more. In the words of one of my favorite pastors, "Let me put Bible on it."

In Matthew 25:1-14, we read the parable of the ten virgins— five wise and five unprepared (my words not the bible). They were all waiting for the bridegroom, but only five brought extra oil for their lamps. When the time came, those without oil scrambled to borrow from the prepared ones. But oil can't be borrowed—not the oil of anointing. In this context, the oil symbolizes more than readiness—it represents being anointed for your assignment. The five who didn't bring oil weren't just unprepared—they weren't positioned for purpose. They tried to show up for something they hadn't spiritually prepared for. They tried to walk into a room they weren't anointed to be in. But the five who brought their oil? They were ready.

Their preparation gave them access. They were in the right place at the right time and entered the feast. And when I think of a feast, I think of abundance, overflow, and divine appointment. The takeaway? Don't wait to borrow what you should've been carrying. We see a similar lesson in Esther's story. She was anointed, but she also took

34

the time to prepare. When the moment arrived, she didn't rely solely on her anointing—she was ready. Because of her preparation, she was able to save her people.

So, the question is: Are you prepared for what you are praying for?

Assessing the Situation with Wisdom and Discernment

Esther's strategic approach was marked by her ability to assess the situation with wisdom and discernment. She understood the dynamics of the Persian court, the king's temperament, and the risks involved in revealing her Jewish identity. In business, wisdom, and discernment are critical to making informed decisions. Gathering information, analyzing the market, and understanding your choices' potential risks and rewards is important. Doing this doesn't mean you should operate in paralysis by analysis but rather by making decisions from a place of knowledge and insight. One of the most practical ways to develop wisdom and discernment is by surrounding yourself with trusted advisors or mentors—I call them my personal board of directors.

There are people in your life who won't just tell you what you want to hear—but they'll tell you the truth. The real, loving, hard truth. Especially in the areas where growth is calling your name.

Who challenges you to elevate?
Who pushes you to walk through doors you're afraid to open?
Who do you call when you need someone to intercede in prayer?
Who gives you solid, godly advice when motherhood feels heavy?

I like to call these people your *Elizabeths*.

In Luke 1, Mary—pregnant with promise and carrying Jesus—went to visit her cousin Elizabeth, who was also expecting. But Elizabeth wasn't just ahead of Mary in pregnancy; she was also ahead in experience, wisdom, and spiritual maturity.

When Mary showed up, something *supernatural* happened. The moment she greeted Elizabeth, the baby inside Elizabeth leaped. That wasn't just a sweet moment between two expecting moms—it was a supernatural encounter.

> It was *confirmation*—Mary *was* chosen.
> It was *activation*—something inside her shifted.
> It was *alignment*—one woman's presence stirred another woman's purpose.

That's what your Elizabeths do.
They don't just support you—they *see* you.
They speak life over your assignment.

They call out what's growing inside you, even when you can't explain it. Your Elizabeths don't covet your calling—they *celebrate* it. Their presence doesn't drain you—it makes your spirit leap. We all carry something—dreams, visions, and ideas, but the people around us can either suppress it or stir it up.

So, take a moment today and ask yourself:

Who are my Elizabeths?

Contrast that with Esther 1: King Xerxes surrounded himself with advisors who didn't speak from wisdom— but ego. When Queen Vashti refused his summons, they fueled his pride, not his purpose. And that one decision made in the heat of the moment had lasting consequences. The lesson in this: Your circle can either birth your destiny or derail it. Surround yourself with people who help you discern the voice of God, not just echo your emotions.

Choose Elizabeths—not enablers. Your personal board of directors should do more than simply agree with you; they should offer different perspectives, challenge your assumptions, and provide guidance based on their experiences. Above all, never let your circle replace your Source. Yes, community matters and wise counsel is needed but no voice should ever be louder than God's.

James 1:5 reminds us,

> *"If any of you lacks wisdom, you should ask God, who gives generously to all without finding fault, and it will be given to you."*

God is your ultimate Source of wisdom, and the Holy Spirit is your guide for discernment. Stay connected to Him, and the right voices will always surround you.

Seizing Opportunities

Esther's strategic plan was not only about courage; it was also about timing. She recognized that waiting for the right moment was just as important as taking action. Can you imagine what it would feel like to discover that there was a plot to wipe out your entire family—and you were included? How would you respond? Would you run? Stay silent to protect yourself? Or would you rise with courage, knowing your voice could change everything?

This was Esther's reality. She didn't just hear about a threat—she was part of the target. She had a choice to make: protect her comfort or step into her calling. Just like Esther, there will be moments in our lives when fear knocks on the door—but purpose pushes us to answer anyway. Instead of rushing to reveal Haman's evil plot to the king, she took the time to prepare. And when the moment came for her to go before the King, she didn't hesitate. She spoke with boldness, clarity, and intentionality. Here's what she said:

"Go, gather together all the Jews who are in Susa, and fast for me. Do not eat or drink for three days, night or day. I and my attendants will fast as you do. When this is done, I will go to the king, even though it is against the law. And if I perish, I perish." – Esther 4:16 (NIV)

That wasn't a statement born out of fear—it was a declaration of faith. A posture of full surrender. Esther was saying, *"If this cost me my life, so be it." But even more than that, she was willing to give up the status she had obtained.*

Let's not forget—Esther had become queen. She had access, influence, and favor in the most powerful empire of her time. Yet she was willing to lay all of that on the line. She didn't just risk her life—she risked her position, comfort, and the security that came with her crown. Purpose meant more than privilege, and obedience outweighed status. That's the kind of bold obedience we're being called into. The kind that says, "I'm willing to lose what I've gained— even if it means honoring God's assignment on my life —then let it be so." You may not be facing a king or a throne, but every purpose-driven woman will come to a crossroad: Will I protect my comfort or pursue my calling?

Opportunities in life rarely come wrapped in perfection. They show up unexpectedly quiet, subtle, and sometimes even inconvenient.

That's why being prepared to move when the right opportunity comes is just as important as the opportunity itself. It's a balancing act between planning and execution, waiting and walking, wisdom and faith. Sometimes, God shifts our plans—not to frustrate us, but to realign us with His purpose.

Proverbs 19:21 puts it plainly:

"Many are the plans in a person's heart, but the LORD's purpose prevails."

Girl—I know this all too well. I'm a planner's planner like a print-the-itinerary, label-the-folders, check-the-boxes kind of planner. My kids know that if they want to go somewhere, they better come with a full report: Who's going? What time? Where at? What's the plan after? (And I need at least a 24-hour notice—minimum.)

Honestly, it's a gift…but it can also be a problem. Planning gives me a sense of control—and faith often requires me to release it. My husband jokes that this is exactly why he waits to tell me things—he knows my brain will go into logistics mode immediately. And he's not wrong!

What I've come to realize is this: God works with us in the way He knows we'll understand. And sometimes, that means not giving us the full picture up front—because if He did, we'd try to edit the plan. Faith isn't about having all the details. It's about trusting that even when the details are missing, God isn't.

There have been seasons of transition in my life where I felt like I was walking in the dark. Not because God wasn't speaking, but because He knew me too well. He knew that if the plan didn't make sense to me upfront, I'd overthink it, question it—or worse—resist it. Let me tell you about the time I was preparing for a business trip to Toronto. Now you already know—your girl wanted all the details. Flight info, agenda, hotel plans, outfits…the whole itinerary.

But no matter how much I tried to lock it all in, I kept hitting walls. I was so frustrated, I almost canceled the trip. Not because I wasn't ready to go but because I didn't have control. And isn't that how we treat God sometimes? We say we trust Him, but the moment He leaves out a detail, we panic. Now, as I sit here writing this, I'm laughing because it reminds me of buckling my daughter in the car; she's in the backseat asking, "Where are we going? How long will it take? Who's going to be there? Will I be able to get something?" As if she's the one paying for the trip!

Just like her, I wanted every single detail before I moved. I'm so grateful for a Father who knows our temperament, our tendencies, and our triggers. And won't change His plans for us regardless of our feelings or lack of action. We act like obedience requires the full blueprint but only requires a yes. But looking back, I realize—God was protecting my peace by stretching my patience and my dependence on him. God designed us to walk with Him, to trust Him fully, and to know that His plans far exceed anything we could orchestrate on our own. So, sis, when God calls, don't hesitate. Step forward in faith, knowing that He is walking with you.

It reminds me of that viral reel going around that says, "Get somebody else to do it." Well, let me tell you—we serve a God who won't hesitate to do just that if we don't step up! Do you remember when Mordecai reminded Esther of this? When she first hesitated to help the Jews, he told her straight up, "If you keep silent at this time, relief and deliverance for the Jews will arise from another place . . . But who knows? *"Perhaps you were born for such a time as this" (Esther 4:14)*

We've all experienced moments of arrogance when God asks us to do something, and we think we're the only ones who can handle it—as if God needs us. The truth is, we should be in awe that God entrusts us with the task of carrying out His will, despite our flaws. So, here's the lesson: Trust the process—even when the picture isn't clear. Obedience isn't about having all the details. It's about trusting that the One who called you already knows the way. And not only that—He's already placed within you everything you need to make an impact: your gifts, your strengths, and yes—even your weaknesses.

It's humbling—almost overwhelming—to realize that the God of the universe who took His time to map out every detail of your life with the same intentionality He used to shape the stars and speak the world into existence. When we allow God to use us, we reach levels that make people wonder, "How did that even happen? "To the natural eye, you may look unqualified—not enough experience, not the best credit score, not enough followers but let me remind you: BUT GOD.

When God steps in and assigns a task to you, He also delegates the authority to accomplish it. This means while you are entrusted with the assignment, the ultimate responsibility for the outcome rests with the One who assigned it—GOD.

Translation? GOD NEVER FAILS.

So, the real question is: Are you going to say yes to what God is calling you to do, or will He have to "get somebody else to do it" Because He will. Now if that stung a little bit—good. Conviction is a sign that God loves you and is calling you higher. You were not created for mediocrity. You weren't meant to just scroll through life— yes, I said scroll—watching others walk in purpose while you stay stuck on the sidelines. When God strategically positions you, failure isn't even part of the equation.

We often confuse preparation with progress and sit on God-given ideas—waiting for perfect conditions, flawless execution, or a sign that we are on the right track. And while we're *planning* to obey— which is not the same as *actually* obeying—we watch someone else launch the very thing that we talk about doing.

Sis, let this hit your spirit: God gave *you* that idea for a reason.

He trusted *you* with that vision. You were called to create, to build, to lead—with boldness, not busyness or hesitation. This is your reminder:

You don't need another sign.
You don't need another degree.
You don't need to wait for perfect.
You just need to say YES—and move.

Stop rehearsing the plan when it's time to walk it out. Your impact doesn't begin when it's perfect; it begins when you obey. I remember when God put it on my heart to start a YouTube channel. The first thing I did? I dove straight into the details—finding the perfect banner, figuring out an intro, updating my profile picture, brainstorming the ideal name, and even planning a trailer. You know what? That channel was doomed from day one because I was focused on appearance, not assignment. I wanted the right camera, the perfect lighting, the trending topics... But I never asked the *Creator* what He wanted *created*.

And now? Ask me how many subscribers I have. At the time of writing this book, I have exactly: ZERO. That's right. Zero subscribers. Not because I didn't have the skill or the passion—But because I never *surrendered* the vision.

When I finally started writing this book, I pulled out all my planners—The ones filled with goals, deadlines, business ideas, and "dream life" blueprints— And I laid them down at God's feet.

I said, "Lord, step into my business the way You stepped onto Peter's boat." I didn't just want Him to bless my strategy—I wanted Him to be the strategy.

And I can already hear your thoughts:
"I'm tired."
"I've been trying."
"I don't want to get it wrong again."

Sis, I feel you. But let me tell you this—your tiredness doesn't disqualify you. It might just be God's cue to take the lead. We truly honor God when we steward our gifts, talents, roles, and responsibilities His way. Colossians 3:23 reminds us, *"Whatever you do, work heartily, as for the Lord and not for men."*

A big part of protecting your gift is learning to prioritize it. That means being intentional about where you invest your time, energy, and resources—and being willing to say no to anything that doesn't align with your purpose or capacity. It's not just about jobs or positions—it's also about relationships, commitments, and connections. Who you're yoked with matters.

We all desire to see fruit in our lives. But here's the truth: Fruit doesn't just manifests, it's the result of deliberate care—the right soil, consistent watering, and necessary pruning. Just like in nature, the type of fruit you bear depends on where you're planted and who you're growing with. When He starts removing people from your life, don't chase after what He's trying to free you from. Real growth only happens when you're rooted in the right environment, surrounded by people who nurture—not drain—your calling.

Are you connected to a home church where you're spiritually fed, or are you trying to thrive in toxic, dry soil? If your environment isn't feeding your spirit, your growth will be stunted. How much "Son" time are you getting? Just as a tree needs sunlight to grow, we need Jesus, the Son, to thrive. Are you truly spending time in prayer, worship, and studying the Word, or are you just going through the motions?

Are you being nourished? What are you consuming daily? Are you filling your mind with wisdom, faith, and encouragement, or are you absorbing negativity and distractions? Remember, whatever you nourish will grow. Matthew 7:18 reminds us, "A good tree cannot produce bad fruit, nor can a bad tree produce good fruit." So, what kind of fruit are you bearing? If you're constantly struggling, feeling drained, or stuck, it might be time to examine your soil, your "Son" time, and your nourishing habits. You can't expect an apple tree harvest if you're feeding yourself like an orange tree.

The Power of Being Yoked with the Right People

Your fruit is a reflection of your connections. Proverbs 27:17 reminds us, "As iron sharpens iron, so one person sharpens another." The right partnerships will refine you, challenge you, and keep you aligned with God's purpose. Let's be real—when you stay connected to people who aren't spiritually aligned, it doesn't just drain you... it distracts you. It pulls you out of position and, even worse, it dulls your discernment. Now, let me keep it all the way real—I haven't always been this way. There were seasons when I was so focused on my own agenda only to be met with frustration and confusion—wondering why nothing was bearing fruit.

Then it hit me—God wanted to do something in my life, but first, I had to break some unhealthy yokes. Breaking those connections was a form of protection. Elevation requires separation. And sometimes, obedience feels like outgrowing the circles that once felt comfortable. Not everyone is assigned to your next chapter—and that's okay. Let them go, so you can grow. I personally had to take an honest look in the mirror and recognize the deeper issues: People Pleasing, Seeking Validation, and Selfish Ambition.

Now don't get me wrong—there's nothing wrong with setting goals or striving for excellence. But when you're checking every box, chasing every opportunity, and saying "yes" to prove your worth, you end up burned out, empty,exhausted and unfulfilled. And no one is giving out the—burnout badge of the year. When I found my identity in Christ, I began to release the things that were never meant for me. And guess what? "No" became my new secret weapon.

Once we recognize that our gifts are meant to serve God's kingdom rather than ourselves, saying no becomes much easier. God doesn't want us running on empty. He calls us to operate in excellence, and you can't do that when you're stretched too thin. God is calling you to examine your soil, relationships, and priorities because when you're properly planted, your fruit will be abundant.

So, take a moment to ask yourself:

Am I planted in good soil?

Who am I yoked with—are they sharpening me or dulling me?

Is my fruit a reflection of my faith, or am I struggling to grow?

God loves us so much that He understands our capacity better than we do. That's why He calls us to seek Him. Seek Him daily to be filled, seek Him when making decisions, and seek Him for clarity because He sees the complete picture, even when we cannot fathom what's next. When we try to keep up with societal pressures, we commit to things that were never a part of God's plan. We strive, and grind—And for what?

"What good is it for someone to gain the whole world, yet forfeit their soul?"

– Mark 8:36 (NIV)

Sis—if the hustle is costing you your peace, compromising your purpose, or causing you to lose sight of who you are in Christ… it's too expensive. There comes a point in our journey when we get tired of just doing good things—and begin to hunger for the God things. We shift from striving in our own strength to moving in divine alignment. We're no longer driven by productivity or performance. This is the moment when God's vision for our lives begins to unfold—not just *around* us, but *through* us. It starts showing up in our decisions, our relationships, and even our mindset. God knows the weight we carry, the moments we question if it's worth it, and how easy it is to lose heart right in the middle of the process. That's why He didn't just give us instructions—He gave us His Word as comfort, as an anchor, and as a promise. One of those promises reminds us that our work is not in vain Galatians 6:9 (ESV)

"Let us not grow weary in well-doing, for in due season we will reap, if we do not give up."

45

It's a reminder that the middle is not the end. This scripture has carried me through so many seasons of waiting and wondering. While the timing may not always be ours to control, the harvest is guaranteed—if we don't quit. And when we feel like we've got nothing left to give, we can hold onto this truth:

> *"But those who wait on the Lord shall renew their strength; they shall mount up with wings like eagles, they shall run and not be weary, they shall walk and not faint." – Isaiah 40:31 (NKJV)*

I keep these verses on my vision board to remind me that in due season, I will reap. And guess what, sis? So will you. Through it all, God promises to renew our strength—if we wait on Him. In our pursuit of goals, we must not put them before the One who orchestrates our paths. Our steps are ordered by the Lord, which reveals that God, by nature, is a strategist, and we are part of His strategic plan. The goal is to align our strategies with God's purpose for our lives. When we do, we experience His guidance and favor in ways we never imagined—because we're no longer striving outside of our design but operating fully within it.

While God is the ultimate strategist—masterfully orchestrating purpose, seasons, and outcomes—He has also entrusted us with the power of choice. Scripture reminds us that *"faith without works is dead"* (James 2:17), emphasizing that although God orders our steps, it's still our responsibility to take them. We are not passive participants in His plan—we are active partners. Our decisions, our discipline, and our daily obedience matter. God may open the door, but we must walk through it. He may give direction, but we must choose to move.

In this partnership, our choices become the vehicle through which His will is carried out in our lives. When strategy meets obedience, that's when God shows up and shows out. So sis, Keep sowing. Keep showing up. Your harvest is on the way.

Prayer for Strategic Preparation

Father God,

Thank You for the divine assignments You have placed on my life, even when I don't always feel qualified to carry them. Help me prepare my heart, hands, and mind for everything You have called me to. Teach me to pause and seek You first before making any decisions. Remind me that strategy without You is just busyness, but my plans are established and anointed through You. Lord, break every spirit of distraction, doubt, and comparison that tries to pull me away from what You have assigned me to do. Surround me with the right people, fill me with divine wisdom, and give me the boldness to act when the time is right. I don't want to build solely for myself—I want to build for Your Kingdom. Align my steps with Your purpose and help me walk in faith, courage, and strategic excellence, just like Esther.

In Jesus' name,

Amen

Reflection Questions:

1. What plans, dreams, or projects do you need to surrender to God right now, trusting Him to establish the next steps?
2. Where have you been rushing or moving impulsively, and how can you slow down to create a plan rooted in diligence and wisdom? What resources, support, or boundaries do you need to put in place to sustain what you're building?
3. How can you invite God's purpose to take the lead and shift your focus from good ideas to God ideas?

Scriptures for Meditation

1. Jeremiah 29:11 (NIV) *"For I know the plans I have for you,"* *declares the Lord, "plans to prosper you and not to harm you, plans to give you a hope and a future."*

2. Ecclesiastes 3:1 (NIV) *"There is a time for everything, and a season for every activity under the heavens."*

3. Proverbs 24:3-4 (NIV) *"By wisdom a house is built, and through understanding it is established; through knowledge its rooms are filled with rare and beautiful treasures."*

4. Romans 8:28 (NIV) *"And we know that in all things God works for the good of those who love him, who have been called according to his purpose."*

Declaration for Strategic Preparation

I decree and declare that my preparation is not in vain.

I align my plans with God's purpose and trust that He is establishing every step I take. I release the need to rush.

I embrace diligence, strategy, and divine timing over busyness and burnout.

I believe that the plans God has for me are filled with hope, purpose, and prosperity.

I prepare not just for today but for the future He has already secured.

I count the cost with wisdom. I build with intention.

I steward the vision with excellence.

I release my own agenda and surrender to God's perfect will.

I believe that His purpose will always prevail in my life.

I am a woman of strategy.

I am a woman of discernment.

I am a woman of divine preparation. And with Esther Energy, I step forward— Bold, Focused, and Ready.

In Jesus' name,

Amen

TRANSFORM

"Do not conform to the pattern of this world, but be transformed by the renewing of your mind. Then you will be able to test and approve what God's will is—His good, pleasing and perfect will."

—Roman 12:2

Girl, let's talk about trusting God in those transition seasons—especially when you're standing at your own Red Sea, waiting for it to split... and nothing happens. You know the kind of season I mean—when you're doing all the right things, praying the bold prayers, showing up with faith, and still... silence. No sudden breakthrough. Just waves in front of you and pressure behind you.

It's one thing to trust God when the doors swing wide open. But it's a whole other level when you're waiting for waters to part, and all you hear is *"be still."* That's the kind of faith that builds endurance. That's the kind of trust that's not based on what you see, but *who you know God to be.* Take a page from Queen Esther's story. She trusted God's purpose for her life—even when the weight of an entire nation rested on her obedience. Imagine being in her shoes: a young woman taken from her home and thrust into what was essentially an ancient beauty pageant. She was judged, adorned, and presented before a king—told to hide her true identity—and then suddenly called to risk everything to save her people. Talk about a transition season.

During transition, we can often feel alone but God will always send you a helper in your transition season. For Esther, it was the head eunuch who gave her favor, wisdom, and access in the palace—and it was Mordecai, her trusted voice of truth, who reminded her of her purpose when fear tried to paralyze her.

God never calls you to something without placing the right people around you. They may not always look like what you expect—but they'll carry the insight, support, or strategy you need for that season. Sometimes, they help you navigate the unfamiliar. Other times, they help you remember who you are when you forget.

When you're in a transition season—whether it's stepping into motherhood, changing jobs, starting a business, or just navigating the unknown—it's easy to feel like you need to control every little detail. However, it's having a posture that says, *"God, I don't know how this is all going to turn out, but I'm trusting You—because You know better than I do."* It's remembering that your God-given purpose is bigger than you can see now. We serve a God who equips us for the future and loves us enough to be present with us in the moment. Right now, at this very moment, He is already working behind the scenes—aligning circumstances, opening doors, closing others, and positioning you exactly where you need to be. And yet, we still try to figure it all out on our own. But let me tell you, sis—true trust is stepping back and admitting, "I can't do it all, and that's okay."

Just like Esther leaned on Mordecai and her circle, we are called to lean on the people God has placed in our lives. The hardest part of trusting God isn't just believing He will come through; it's having patience while we wait. It's trusting His timing even when everything in you screams, "Hurry up, God!" Look at Esther—she didn't walk into the king's court without fear, but that didn't hold her back. She understood the weight of that moment

It reminded me of a widely circulated image on the Internet: a little girl standing with Jesus, clutching her small teddy bear while He gently gestures for her to hand it over. She doesn't realize that behind His back, He is holding something much bigger. That's exactly how God is with us. He's saying, "Give it to Me. Surrender it. Trust Me, and I will fulfill the desires of your heart." However, too often, we hold on to what's comfortable, what we understand, and what feels safe, not realizing that God's plans for us are beyond what we can imagine.

We love to pray, "Lord, show me how good it can get." But you can't receive what God has for you while still clutching what He's asking you to release. Remember in the first chapter when I talked about getting pregnant unexpectedly? Let me set the scene before that happened. It was September 5th when I got my DD-214 from the U.S. Navy. I officially hung up my Navy Chief hat to put my family first after serving 21 years.

But what followed wasn't exactly the peaceful transition I'd imagined. Little did I know, this unexpected plot twist would ignite a journey of self-discovery, testing the boundaries of my strength, resilience, and the very essence of who I thought I was. But you know what we do when something epic happens, right? Girl, we post it!

I took this beautiful picture with the backdrop of the sky, all perfect with blue and fluffy clouds, and posted it with the caption: DD-214 received, now on to creating a legacy, and I went to the Secretary of State of Texas to file for my free LLC to do just that. Did I have a clue what being an entrepreneur meant? Nope. Did I know what kind of services I'd provide? Not a chance. I was diving in headfirst with zero plans. But before the journey began, I had the opportunity to interview for what I thought would be my dream job. Executive Assistant to the General Manager of the Spurs. Yep, you read that right, the NBA San Antonio Spurs.

Talk about a moment where you think, *Is this happening*? I remember walking into that building, nerves on high, and as I was waiting to be called back, I caught a glimpse of Coach Popovich himself. The security guard casually mentioned I was interviewing for a position being vacated because the current assistant was being promoted. *I can't believe I'm even here!* kept running through my mind. I went through the interview feeling like they were going to end it by saying, "You will receive an email with your official job offer within the hour." However, days went by, and no call came. Here's the thing—I've always had a strong sense of discernment.

Something in me whispered You didn't get it. I remember stepping into the shower, crying, thanking God for the opportunity, and surrendering it all to His will. Just as I was getting out of the shower, my phone rang. It was the General Manager himself calling.

Now, you know the Human Resource Department usually calls with news, good or bad, but this was different. He told me how impressed he was and how hard it was to decide; however, they were going in a different direction.

I was so overwhelmed, just grateful that he took the time to call me personally. Y'all, I hung up and broke down again, but this time it was different. I could almost hear God say, "Well done, daughter but I have something else for you."

That's when my journey into the wilderness really began. Back then, I couldn't understand why things were happening the way they were. Looking back now, it's like following breadcrumbs—each moment of provision, every bit of pruning, all of it was building my faith for what was to come. Now this is the part that I didn't think I was ready for. It started with a frantic call to my best friend. "Hey, Shell (short for Michelle)," I whispered nervously, "my friend hasn't come to town yet." Every woman knows this is code for "my period hasn't come." Her reply was so reassuring. "Give it a couple of days," she said confidently. "It will come."

Honestly, I don't know why her response eased my nerves, but it did. I'm giggling as I think about how much water I drank over the next few days, as if it would somehow make my period arrive faster. Fast forward to my husband yelling at the television during the Army Navy game, completely oblivious that I was in the bathroom waiting for the results of a pregnancy test. To my total disbelief, the result was PREGNANT. Instant denial washed over me. It had only been four months since I retired! I could hear Shell shouting over the phone, *"Girl, you are married with kids already; it's going to be okay."*

I had so many plans after retirement, and being pregnant at 40 was not one of them. I patiently waited for Ashton Kutcher to pop out and tell me I was being "Punked." After taking three more secret pregnancy tests, it was finally time to tell my husband. I grabbed an Amazon box from the garage, slid the pregnancy test inside, and handed it to him. You might be wondering—why an Amazon box? Well, his love language is gifts, and let's just say... I had a *very* special gift on the way.

He opened it with that familiar childlike excitement, thinking it was something off his Amazon Wishlist. But then—his expression shifted. That smile turned into wide-eyed silence. Pure shock. He just stared at it. At that moment, I knew this was the beginning of a whole new chapter—for both of us.

Deep down, I was terrified. As much as I wanted to celebrate the news, fear had already crept in. After three miscarriages and the devastating loss of a baby later in pregnancy, I couldn't help but brace for the worst. I didn't want to hear those words again: *"I'm sorry, there's no heartbeat."* If you've ever heard those words, you know how they change you. Time slows, the room spins, and the tears refuse to stop. It's a silence that lingers so heavily, you don't even know if you're still breathing. It pierces you in a way that only time and God can heal. The most recent miscarriage happened the day after Mother's Day.

We looked like the picture-perfect little sitcom family—Mom, Dad, a boy and a girl in tow. We walked into that appointment full of joy, already imagining what life would look like with one more heartbeat in the mix.

Our kids were giggling in the waiting room, arguing over snacks. We were glowing. And then, everything changed. I walked out holding more pain than I knew how to process. No heartbeat. Just the weight of having to tell two sweet little faces that *Mommy's not having a baby after all.* There's no script for that kind of heartbreak.

Fast forward two years later... I'm sitting in my gynecologist's office, arms crossed, heart guarded, practically demanding that she order lab tests for a blood draw—because there was *no way* I could be pregnant. I was in complete denial. After all the loss... all the grief... all the questions I had shoved deep down in prayer and silence—I had trained my heart not to get too hopeful. Here I was, back in the same office with the same walls and fluorescent lights, but a different story began to unfold.

I will never forget her words: *"Sure thing, but just so you know, I had my baby at 40, and you will too."* At the time, I was 39 years old and already had three kids. My husband was preparing to leave for a job assignment in Killeen, three hours away from our home in San Antonio. Living apart felt like the worst decision we could have made, but it was our reality.

If you think I'm about to say everything got easier with prayer — think again. I cried at the front door more mornings than I can count, especially on Sundays, watching my husband pull away, knowing I wouldn't see him again until the following Friday. I built routines for the kids—not because I had it all figured out, but because I was grasping for some kind of normal, hoping they wouldn't feel the full weight of their father's absence. And I did it all while managing a high- risk pregnancy—trying to hold it all together, even as everything around me felt like it was quietly coming undone. Smiling in public, crying in silence, and praying for peace while bracing for bad news.

That season stretched me more than any had before— spiritually, emotionally, and physically. It's that type of test that exposes everything you thought you had under control. To make matters worse, all of this was unfolding as the world was literally shutting down. But I distinctly remember the moment I surrendered it all to God. I was in the nurse's office, waiting to receive my glucose test results.

I'm sitting in the nurse's office, a space that felt surprisingly welcoming and peaceful. With a calm and gentle voice, she said, *"Your glucose results came back, and unfortunately, they're much higher than we'd like. This isn't something we can manage with diet alone—you'll need to start giving yourself insulin shots twice a day."* I sat there, in shock.

Although I knew that gestational diabetes wasn't my fault, I couldn't help feeling like I was failing already. Tears ran down my face; the nurse looked me in the eyes, and said, *"Honey, you didn't do anything wrong. And we're going to do everything we can to make sure you and this baby and you are okay."* At that moment, I let go. I stopped trying to micromanage what only God could carry.

That was the moment I surrendered—not just my pregnancy, but my fear, my need to have it all together, and the illusion of control. Somehow, in releasing it, I found peace. I let go of the fear of miscarriages and began to thank God for what He was doing. I declared that I would deliver a healthy and whole baby without any complications.

Amazing things happen when you yield to God. A level of protection, provision, and favor surrounds you and those connected to you. While there was turmoil across the country due to the pandemic, my family remained covered. And let me tell you—trusting God was not optional.

At 6½ months pregnant, the Army sent my husband to Poland. Now, all I could do was pray that I would have someone here with me if I went into labor early because I still had three kids at home.

Due to Covid restrictions, only one person was allowed in the delivery room—and they had to have a negative Covid test. I remember crying on the phone to my best friend, overwhelmed and unsure of what I was going to do. Thankfully, my husband's unit arranged for him to come home. But when he arrived, the doctor made it clear: he had to test negative for Covid to be present for labor and delivery.

It was the first time I had ever seen him nervous. After traveling through three countries just to get home, he stood there—visibly anxious. He didn't want to miss the birth of our baby, but he was also concerned about the risk of our family getting sick, especially since we have two children with asthma. "*Mr. Leftridge, your test is negative.*"

Ava Simone was born the same month I posted about creating a legacy with an LLC. It hadn't even been a year yet . . . God has a sense of humor that makes you laugh when others would be crying. He was thinking of legacy in another way. Trust is more than just a nice word; it's an action. It's believing God is still in control even when things don't make sense. Sis, I need you to trust that your transition season is leading to elevation.

The 5 Ps of Elevation

Posture. Pruning. Preparation. Positioning. Promotion.

When I became a Chief Petty Officer, I participated in a training program called "Transition." Active and retired Chiefs shared their wisdom, experience, and guidance for six intense weeks with us. This culminated in what we referred to as "Final Night."

After all the training, lessons, and challenges, it marked the moment of our acceptance into the Chief's Mess—a true culmination of our preparation and readiness. Like my Navy training, advancing to the next level requires a blend of preparation, wisdom, and intentionality.

Elevation doesn't happen accidentally it's a deliberate, and is often an uncomfortable process. Growth that lasts is rarely easy. It requires surrender, discipline, and a willingness to be stretched beyond what feels safe. We all want the blessing…but we don't always like the *stretching* that comes before it.

That's why the 5 Ps of Elevation are so important. These five phases aren't just steps—they're designed to build your character and strength. Oftentimes, we get stuck in a phase—not because God isn't moving, but because of the resistance we give Him. We pray for the increase but hesitate when the process begins to refine us. However, elevation requires capacity, and capacity involves pruning.

You can't carry more without letting go of what no longer serves the next season.

Let's break them down:

1. Posture: The Heart Check

Before God elevates us, He continuously checks the posture of our hearts. He's not focused on our résumé, reputation, or how much we've accomplished—He's looking at our willingness to surrender. Are we aligned with His will or are we still chasing our own? This is where God invites us to shift from striving to submitting, to lay down our agendas and make room for His. Elevation always starts in the secret place—with humility, obedience, and a heart willing to say, "Yes, Lord," even when it's uncomfortable. Because the posture of our heart determines how we're positioned. And if we're not submitted in private, the weight of the next level will only expose what we haven't surrendered or healed from in public.

2. Pruning: The Cut-Off

After posture comes pruning. This is the phase where God begins to cut away everything that can't go with us to the next level—old habits, unhealthy relationships, limiting beliefs, and outdated mindsets. At first, it feels like a loss. It may even feel like rejection. But in reality, God is making space for what's coming. Pruning isn't punishment—it's preparation disguised as pain. This phase challenges us to trust God's *no* just as much as His *yes*, and to believe that what feels like a setback is actually a setup for greater fruit.

3. Preparation: The Behind-the-Scenes Work

Preparation is the phase where God does the deep, behind-the-scenes work in us. It's where He equips us with the discipline, wisdom, and resilience needed to carry the weight of where we're headed. Most of this work happens in private—far from the spotlight, without applause or recognition. It's not glamorous, but it's necessary. In this season, God sharpens our gifts, develops our character, and stretches our faith. He's not just pouring into us—He's building something within us that will last. Remember, elevation without preparation doesn't lead to promotion—it leads to pressure we're not ready for. And God loves us too much to send us unprepared.

4. Positioning: The Divine Alignment

In the positioning phase, God begins to place you in rooms you never imagined you'd enter. Doors start opening—ones you couldn't have forced open if you tried. But this is where discernment becomes crucial. You must be able to recognize the difference between a divine shift and a distraction in disguise. God begins to align you with people, places, and opportunities that are directly connected to your purpose. But here's the catch: He doesn't always position you where it's comfortable—He places you where you'll be most effective. And more often than not, you won't feel "ready." But positioning is never about how prepared *you* feel—it's about how prepared *God* knows you are.

Promotion: The Release Into the Promise

This is the part we all pray for—the breakthrough, the blessing, the moment everything aligns. But let's be honest: you can't skip to promotion without first going through the process. Promotion without pruning leads to pride. Elevation without preparation leads to burnout. But when your posture is surrendered, your pruning embraced, your preparation complete, and your heart stays open in the positioning—*then* God releases the promotion that's had your name on it all along. What sets this apart from a worldly promotion is simple: it's not just for you. Kingdom promotion is always connected to purpose. It's designed to impact others, to serve well, and ultimately, to glorify God.

Just like the weather shifts with the seasons, our spiritual lives go through seasons, too. Ecclesiastes reminds us, *"To everything there is a season, and a time for every purpose under heaven."* (Ecclesiastes 3:1). That means your process has a purpose—even if it doesn't align with your calendar.

So, sis, don't base your goals solely on the time of year. Don't rush ahead just because the world says it's "your season." Instead, ask yourself: *What spiritual phase am I in right now?*

Is God checking your posture?
Pruning something away?
Preparing you in private?
Positioning you in unexpected places?

Seasons of transition aren't times of stagnation. Remember, before God elevates you to the next level, He ensures you're *spiritually, mentally, and emotionally ready.*

I'll never forget what a Master Chief once told me: *"When you put on the hat of a Chief Petty Officer, you become the answer."* That's why the Navy says, *"Ask the Chief."* You're the solution before the question is even asked. Similarly, when God takes us through a transition, he positions us to be the answer for someone else's prayers. Sometimes, God confirms you're not alone in your becoming by placing someone on your path who's walking through it too.

Let me share a moment that started as small talk but was a shift in disguise. I invited her on as a guest for what was supposed to be a regular podcast episode—questions, conversation, wrap-it-up. But after we hit "stop" on the recording, we kept talking. Just a casual conversation about life, motherhood, and what God we were doing behind the scenes. Thirty minutes in, it was clear —this wasn't just a conversation. Something had shifted. It felt like we'd known each other for years. Not on a surface-level, "we've got stuff in common" way—but in that rare, *heart-level connection* that makes you realize this moment was never random. Our paths didn't just cross—they collided with purpose. And almost in sync, we both said, *"Girl, I'm in my 'I QUIT' phase."* We laughed—but it was the kind of laugh that comes with a lump in your throat because we both knew exactly what that meant.

We were in that place where everything around seems like its shifting, including the roles, relationships, and routines. Things you thought you needed to hold onto were suddenly gone. The dreams you thought you were chasing felt out of reach. We were in the pruning season. If you've ever been there, you know it can feel like isolation. We realized something as we kept talking, and "girl, me too" moments filled the air. It wasn't isolation; it was consecration. God was stripping things away not to punish us but to position us. He was making space to do something new in our lives. Something we honestly hadn't even been bold enough to pray and ask for.

We were in our individual hidden seasons but walking it out together. Praying for each other, checking in on the hard days, and speaking life when doubt tried to settle in. As the pruning slowed down, God began to process us for the next phase. This is the part where God starts piecing things together but only after you've let some things go. It required us to surrender and release the old, so we could carry the new. When you know you're in God's hands, you don't need the whole map, you just need the next step.

You know that moment at airport security where they tell you to step into the scanner, raise your arms, and stand still? You are a little awkward, vulnerable, and exposed as they check for anything that doesn't belong. That's what it feels like when God processes us through phases. It's like He's saying, "Raise your arms. Surrender. Let Me show you what needs to go and what gets to stay." This part can feel more difficult than pruning because now you're not just losing things—you're being shown things.

God gives you a glimpse of who you really are—not the version that life tried to shape you into, not the version fear tried to shrink, but the real you—the one He intended you to be. And just like at airport security, that posture of surrender reveals the smallest things. When you're lifting your arms to God, say, "Have Your way," and in that stillness, He starts revealing the truth of your identity.

The very gifts the enemy tried to steal are the same ones God plans to use for good. In Esther's story, we see God's presence doesn't always show up in words; sometimes, it's His movement that speaks the loudest. Think back to a time when you didn't feel God, but He moved in a way that left no doubt it was Him.

Maybe you were journaling your heart out, reading Scripture, wondering if God was even listening. Then, out of nowhere, the Holy Spirit whispered something so clear it stopped you in your tracks. And, as if heaven was confirming it in real time, someone spoke the exact words your soul needed. Maybe it was a random conversation that hit a little too deep to be random. Or a sermon that felt like the pastor had somehow read your journal. You know what I'm talking about. Those moments aren't just coincidences.

They're God's way of saying, "I see you. I've never left you. I'm in this with you." Here's the thing—You have to be in position to recognize them. It's not that God isn't moving in our lives. It's that sometimes we're too distracted, too discouraged, or too doubtful to notice. When your heart is open, when your spirit is tuned in, when you're still enough to listen—you'll start to see just how close He really is. I'm reminded of that verse in Isaiah: *"Behold, I am doing a new thing"*

When Moses died, it marked the end of an era. He had led the Israelites through the wilderness, stood before Pharaoh, parted the Red Sea, and carried the weight of an entire nation on his shoulders.

But when it came time to enter the Promised Land, Moses couldn't lead them in.

Enter Joshua—a man of obedience and faith. He was one of only two spies who believed God could deliver on His promise, even when the majority gave in to fear. Joshua trusted what God said, and not what the crowd saw. He had served faithfully under Moses, and when the moment came, he didn't shrink back—he *stepped up.*

And here's what's powerful: God didn't just let Moses die— He buried him in an unknown place.

> *"And He buried him in a valley in the land of Moab... but to this day no one knows the exact place."*

Deuteronomy 34:6 (NLT)

Why? Because God knew the people would be tempted to build shrines around the past. They would've stayed stuck mourning what was instead of moving forward into what could be. No matter how great Moses had been, clinging to him would've kept them from following Joshua—and stepping into the new thing God was doing.

God helped them let go and sis, He still does that with us.

Sometimes we try to carry old identities, roles, or relationships into our next season—but they were only meant to serve us in the *last* one. God loves us enough to remove what can't go with us—not to punish us, but to *prepare* us. God is still in the business of transition.

And when He buries something, it's never to end your story. It's to *resurrect a new one.*

The real challenge in transitions is Trusting the process. We talk a lot about wanting to experience heaven on earth, but that kind of breakthrough requires the right mindset. Look at the Israelites—they didn't just stroll into the Promised Land. God had to shift their perspective before He shifted their position.

If I can be transparent, that's been my prayer lately. "Lord, position me for the Promised Land. Mature me so I won't mismanage the blessing when it comes." Because, if I'm keeping it real I've had my own Israelite seasons. I've been hard-headed, putting things before God. I've gone outside of His will, chasing comfort and control. I've even held onto things I had no business holding onto. But sis . . . can I just tell you how grateful I am for grace?

God will redirect you—even if it means removing people, places, or things that don't align with His plan. This is when the feelings of isolation take a seat at the table. You feel alone and forgotten, as if everything's being stripped away. But what if we reframed that? We see a pattern throughout Scripture: when God was about to transform someone's life, He often got them alone.

Moses was by himself when he encountered the burning bush — and everything about his identity and assignment shifted. Hagar was running, exhausted and overlooked, yet it was in the wilderness— alone—where God saw her and gave her hope. Jacob was isolated, wrestling through the night, and it was in that fight that his name, his future, and his entire identity were changed.

Transformation often happens when were alone, where distractions fade, pride is stripped, and God speaks most clearly. Even when we're at our lowest—He's still speaking. Even when we feel forgotten— He's still faithful. He won't forfeit the plans that he has for us.

Transformation Through Transition

Before Esther wore the crown, she walked through a hidden season that transformed her from an orphaned Jewish girl into the Queen of the most powerful empire of her time. God used that season of preparation to shape her character, deepen her wisdom, and position her for purpose. It wasn't just about beauty treatments or royal protocols—it was a refining process designed to call forth the leader, the intercessor, and the deliverer within her.

And she wasn't alone. God placed the right people in her life at the right time. Mordecai, her cousin and guardian, wasn't just family—he was a God-ordained voice reminding her who she really was. When she doubted herself, he spoke purpose:

"Who knows but that you have come to your royal position for such a time as this?"

Esther 4:14

Even the king's eunuch, Hegai, helped her stand out. None of it was random. God was aligning every piece for her assignment. And the same is true for us. See, transition seasons are never just about the change we can see—they're about the transformation happening in us. That internal work is real elevation.

It's in these refining seasons that God strips away what's familiar, stretches our faith, and surrounds us with the right people—those who see what He sees in us. Friends, mentors, and spiritual sisters who refuse to let us play small. The ones who remind us of our identity when we forget. The ones who call us higher when we start settling.

Transformation requires trust—deep, gritty trust. The kind that holds on when nothing looks like what you prayed for. But, sis, God isn't just preparing the path for you—He's preparing *you* for the path. Let's be honest—transformation rarely *feels* supernatural while it's happening. More often, it feels like a loss. Like letting go of roles, dreams, and identities we once clung to as a status symbol.

Esther had to release everything familiar—her home, her culture, even her name. But in surrendering what she knew, she stepped into something greater. Her obedience didn't just shift her story—it secured her people's future. Sometimes the path to purpose requires us to lay down what's comfortable in order to rise into the position God has prepared for us.

You don't need to feel ready. You just need to be willing.

Here is the truth: If He's calling you forward, then transformation is already underway.

Esther Energy Isn't Flashy. It's Faithful.

This is what Esther Energy looks like: it's not loud or flashy—it's steady. Surrendered. Strategic. It's trusting God behind the scenes, even when you don't see the next step. It's showing up in obedience and letting God use your "yes" to shift the atmosphere.

You were made for this moment—not just to survive transition, but to be transformed by it.

Esther Energy Prayer for Transformation

Father God,

Thank You for being the God of every season—the One who goes before me, walks beside me, and carries me through the unknown. In these moments of transition, when the path feels unclear and the future feels uncertain, remind me that You are doing a new thing. Open my eyes to perceive it. Open my heart to receive it. Help me to release control and surrender fully to Your perfect plan. Give me the courage to let go of what was, so I can step boldly into what is next with confidence and peace. Align my heart with Your will. Align my steps with Your purpose. Align my mind with Your truth. Like Esther, I don't want to move ahead of You, and I don't want to shrink back in fear. I want to walk in full obedience, knowing that my position, my purpose, and my promotion are all part of Your divine design. Lord, as I navigate this season, help me to trust Your timing. Strengthen my faith to believe that even in the waiting, even in the stretching, You are working all things together for my good and Your glory. I declare that I am assigned, aligned, and anointed for such a time as this.

In Jesus' name,

Amen

Reflect and Meditate on Seasons of Transition

Isaiah 43:19 (NIV)

> *"See, I am doing a new thing! Now it springs up; do you not perceive it? I am making a way in the wilderness and streams in the wasteland."*

Reflection:

Transition can often feel like wandering through a wilderness, but this verse reminds us that God is already at work, creating something new, even when we can't see it clearly. He is making a way forward, even in the most uncertain places.

Journal Question:

Where in your life do you sense God is trying to do a new thing, and how can you posture your heart to perceive it?

Proverbs 3:5-6 (NIV)

> *"Trust in the Lord with all your heart and lean not on your own understanding; in all your ways submit to Him, and He will make your paths straight."*

Reflection:

When life feels shaky and unclear, it's easy to cling to our own plans and understanding. But this scripture reminds us that real security comes from total surrender—trusting God with every step and letting Him lead the way.

Journal Question:

What area of your life are you struggling to surrender, and what would it look like to fully trust God with it in this season?

HUMBLE

"Humble yourselves, therefore, under the mighty hand of God so that at the proper time He may exalt you."

1 Peter 5:6 (ESV)

When we think about leaders, we often picture someone at the top—confident, decisive, and calling the shots. You know, the kind of person who's steering the ship while rocking a power suit and making bold moves. And yes, confidence *does* matter. But there's another side to great leadership that often gets overlooked: humility.

Humility is what keeps us grounded. It reminds us that our influence doesn't just come from talent, hustle, or an impressive résumé—it comes from God's power working through us. It's what ensures that when we make decisions for our families, grow our businesses, or step into new roles, we lead with compassion and a heart for others—not just for ourselves. Esther's story is a powerful example of humility in action. Yes, she was a queen. Yes, she had influence. But her strength didn't come from ego or power trips.

She didn't lead with pride—she led with reverence. Esther understood the weight of her position. She knew that her decisions weren't just about her—they would impact an entire nation. It would have been easy to make the story all about herself, but she didn't. Her humility under pressure wasn't a weakness—it was one of her greatest strengths. It allowed her to make God-honoring decisions that served others, not just herself. True leadership isn't about being seen. It's about seeing clearly—and choosing obedience over applause.

This reminds me of a lesson I learned the hard way. I'll never forget my early days in the Navy when I was stationed on the USS Blue Ridge, my first ship assignment. Before reporting to my first ship, my Chief Petty Officer gave me one clear goal: *Get qualified as soon as possible.* For me, that meant earning my Enlisted Surface Warfare Specialist (ESWS) Pin—a major milestone in a Sailor's career. I hit the ground running. During my first underway—which lasted four months—I earned my ESWS pin, led the installation of a new security badge system on the ship, and took on several additional duties outside my job. I was giving it everything I had. I felt like I was on top of my game. But what I didn't realize at the time? Not everyone saw it that way.

I was the only Black woman in my division. And while that fact hadn't been front and center before, it became very obvious during evaluation season. I was shocked to receive the lowest grade on my evaluation—a *Promotable.* Even a Sailor who had failed his fitness test scored higher than I did in points.

There I was, in a division full of white men, working twice as hard—leading, executing, excelling—and still being made to feel like I didn't measure up. That evaluation hit me hard emotionally. It was a humbling moment, to say the least, and if that wasn't enough? Not long after, I found out I was pregnant. This meant I couldn't stay on the ship and would be transferred to a shore duty station in Japan. So much for the vindication I was planning. I felt crushed—like all my hard work had been for nothing.

I was leaving my first ship with a poor evaluation, pregnant, and heading to a new command where I'd have to start all over again. And in my head? I was just another stereotypical Black statistic, pregnant with a "baby daddy." I was drowning in disappointment, frustration, and shame. But what I didn't realize then was that God was about to flip the script in a way I never expected.

When I arrived at my new command, I felt like I had something to prove. My last evaluation left me questioning my worth, my work ethic and whether any of it even mattered. Then my Command Master Chief pulled me aside and gave me a choice:

"You can either fight the evaluation or let it go and move forward."

He promised me a fair shot. And while I wasn't entirely convinced, that moment sparked something in me: a tiny flicker of hope that maybe things could shift. But before I could start fresh, I found out my former Chief had already called ahead—framing me as difficult to work with. It wasn't true, but the narrative was already in the air. So, there I was—pregnant, in a new command, feeling like a complete failure. Despite my fears, frustrations, and feelings of defeat, God was working behind the scenes, guiding me to something better.

On my first day, my department Chief sat me down and made it clear: "I don't want any problems. *I need a hard worker and a team player."*

That was all I needed to hear. From that day on, I put my head down and got to work. I wanted to defend myself. To prove them wrong. To perform my way into their approval. And let's be honest—it's easy to slip into that mindset. To confuse diligence with performance. To hustle, not out of faith, but out of fear. But God challenged me to see the difference.

Working for approval exhausts you.

Working diligently unto the Lord empowers you.

And that's when I saw it firsthand—God's promise in real time: The last shall be first. Three years flew by and when it was time for me to transfer, I had made First Class Petty Officer, earned the highest annual evaluation, and my transfer eval came back with a ranking of Early Promote and a recommendation for Chief Petty Officer.

But the real full-circle moment? That came when that same Senior Chief who pulled me into his office on my first day called me back in. Only this time, it wasn't to set me straight. This time, he looked me in the eyes and said, *"Thank you."* Two simple words, but they meant everything. It was proof that hard work, consistency, and letting God handle the rest is all I needed to do. He acknowledged my hard work and even more surprisingly he apologized. He admitted that when I first arrived, he had made assumptions about me, and he was wrong. In that moment, it all clicked. I could see so clearly how God had redeemed my story. I didn't have to fight every battle with my own strength. I just had to stay faithful, keep showing up, and let God take care of the rest. God always makes a way. That's the thing; we're only responsible for our effort, our attitude, and our consistency. We manage our input, but the outcome is God's business. And trust me, He never gets it wrong.

As women—whether we're moms juggling bedtime routines or CEOs managing boardrooms—we carry a lot. Between client meetings, launch deadlines, family obligations, staff development, and everything in between, it's easy to fall into the trap of thinking we have to be a superwoman just to survive the week.

But let's be real, sis—that's not strength. That's just pride dressed up as perfectionism. True leadership isn't about being the loudest in the room or tackling the biggest project. It's about being self-aware knowing your strengths, owning your deficiencies, and leading from a place of humility, not ego.

So how do we practice humility in our daily lives?

First, understand this: humility isn't weakness—and it's certainly not shrinking. It's not about silencing your voice, doubting your ability or downplaying your brilliance. It's about being grounded in who created you. It's the ability to recognize your value without needing to exalt yourself. It's about knowing that every gift you have is given from God for you to serve, not just to shine. Effective leadership isn't about pretending you have all the answers—it's about creating space to grow, to learn, and to uplift the people around you.

Harvard Business Review reports that humility is one of the most essential traits in effective leadership. Research shows that humble leaders are more self-aware, open to feedback, and create stronger, more collaborative teams. Why? Because humility builds trust. It invites others in, instead of pushing them out.

But here's where many of us get tripped up—we mistake humility as meekness, and meekness as weakness. That's when your confidence takes a hit. We start believing that being humble means staying quiet, small, and out of the way. But that's not humility—that's fear disguised as false humility. True humility doesn't diminish your confidence—it amplifies it. When you lead with humility, you serve your family and team with intention. Instead of expecting everyone to fit into your way of doing things, you meet them where they are. You ask questions, listen well, and celebrate their growth. Don't underestimate your encouragement—it can shift atmospheres and spark confidence in someone who desperately needs it.

Humility also means knowing your worth and your Source—leading from a place of quiet confidence and surrendered strength. Meekness is often mistaken for passivity or insecurity, but biblically, meekness is strength under control—the ability to lead with power, without the need to dominate. It's choosing restraint when you could react, and wisdom when the world expects noise.

There's real danger in confusing meekness with low self-worth—because that's when your confidence begins to suffer. When you see meekness as weakness, you start to retreat instead of shine. You become afraid that your "too much". Humility doesn't diminish your confidence—it *deepens* it. Let your confidence be a reflection of who God says you are—not what people expect you to be. When you lead with that kind of humility, you won't just make an impression—you'll make a *God-sized* impact.

There was a time in my entrepreneurial journey when I thought I had to do everything myself—my way, to my exact standards, no exceptions. And let me tell you, that didn't last long. It was exhausting, unsustainable, and honestly? A fast track to burnout. Thankfully, I fell back on the skills I learned as a Chief Petty Officer, specifically delegation and accountability. That's when I started living by one simple phrase: Trust but verify. Trust that you've equipped others with the tools they need to succeed. Verify that the work is getting done with excellence.

Trying to carry it all alone is a recipe for burnout. And when we isolate ourselves thinking we have to figure it out solo—we walk right into the enemy's trap. God is a God of relationships. We were never meant to do this life or business alone. Whether it's in motherhood, business, or life, we thrive when we build, grow, and lead together. From the very beginning Adam and Eve, Esther and Mordecai—God has always worked through divine connections. It's the same in our lives. Success isn't about how big your team is—it's about the quality of the people around you and, more importantly, your reliance on God.

Take Gideon (Judges 6-7) for example. When God first called him, he was hiding, weighed down by fear and self-doubt. Yet, God didn't call him by his weakness. He called him Mighty Warrior. Gideon couldn't believe it. And honestly? That's just like us. God speaks greatness over our lives, but because we can't see it for ourselves, we hesitate, doubt, and question God. Even in our doubt, God is patient. When Gideon thought he needed 3,000 men to win a battle; God showed him that 300 was more than enough. It was never about having the biggest army or the most resources. It was about showing up, fully aware that God has anointed you to fill a unique space in this world and will call you by name.

He doesn't get frustrated with our insecurities—He covers them with grace. *His strength is made perfect by our weakness* (2 Corinthians 12:9-10) And that word perfect? It doesn't mean flawless, it means

73

complete, whole, lacking nothing. So, when we feel weak, insecure, or unworthy that's exactly where God's supernatural steps in. Not to replace us, but to complete us. You are a beautiful reflection of His Word—made whole, not by striving, but by God's unmerited favor.

Now let's rewind back and look closely at Esther before she ever became queen. We often focus on the moment she stepped into her royal authority, but remember, there was a whole season of preparation leading up to that. Before the crown, before the bold decisions, before the life-altering requests, Esther was just a young woman who had been brought into the king's palace, surrounded by unfamiliar faces and completely unsure of what the future held.

In that environment, it would've been so easy to get caught up in the competition—trying to outshine the other women, strutting around like she deserved the crown more than anyone else because of beauty. But that wasn't Esther's style. Instead, she listened, observed, and took advice from those who knew the ropes. Esther didn't rely on her beauty or her own understanding; she humbly accepted the wisdom of those placed around her like the eunuch Hegai, who provided guidance on what pleased the king. Esther's humility reflected her heart and her trust in God's purpose.

She understood that her destiny didn't rest solely in her personal efforts, charisma, or beauty. Her strength was in her surrender. She didn't force her way into purpose—she yielded to it.

This hits close to home for me. Remember when I told you I found out I was pregnant and had to leave the ship? It might sound like just another chapter in my journey, but for me, it was monumental—a moment that completely turned my world upside down. I can pinpoint the exact moment as a teenager when I decided that having children would be the absolute worst decision I could ever make.

When I was about 13, I struggled with terrible menstrual cramps. The lively, energetic version of me would disappear as I lay in bed, curled up miserable in the fetal position. One day, during one of those episodes where I was doubled over in pain from severe cramps, my aunt suddenly burst into my room and said something I'll never forget: *"You better not get pregnant, because if you do, you and that baby are out of here."*

I was in shocked and disbelief really. I wasn't even sure what hurt more: the physical pain or the emotional gut punch of her words. Confused and completely taken aback, I barely whispered, *"I just have cramps."* Her only response? She handed me a hot water bottle and walked away.

I laid there crying—not because of the cramps, but because once again, it was clear that I was seen as nothing more than a burden. Just a check. Just a problem to be managed. The kind of love that corrects with care I didn't know that. What I did know were slaps, whippings, and harsh words—like I was the worst child in the world.

And to make matters worse, no one had ever talked to me about sex, relationships, or even basic understanding of my body. Yet after that accusation, something stuck. Something shifted. That day, I made a vow to myself: I would never have kids. Not because I didn't believe in family—but because, to me, children represented pain, struggle, and rejection. I couldn't imagine bringing life into the world when I wasn't even sure what love looked like.

How could I offer something I'd never truly received?

So, when I found out I was pregnant at 25, it felt like the end of the world. I was in the Navy, living on my own, and was successful by many standards. Yet, none of that mattered. I couldn't fathom how I would go on.

Desperate for validation, I called that same aunt who raised me, the only mother figure I knew. I just needed her to tell me it would be okay. Instead, her response crushed me: "By who? Why are you calling me? My kids don't even give me these problems. "Shocked, I hung up

75

the phone and cried. I felt so lost and empty, even as life was growing inside of me. To make it worse, I couldn't ignore the hypocrisy.

Her son had become a teenage father, and she was actively raising his child. That's when it hit me; I was just her niece, not her child. I wasn't entitled to the same love, support, or protection. That realization reminded me of God's love for us. When we accept Jesus as our Savior, we gain access to a love, favor, and protection that the outside world might see as unfair. It's a love that sets us apart, an undeserved yet unconditional love that carries us through our lowest moments.

Here I was, at a new command, pregnant by a man I didn't see a future with—a man I was honestly ashamed to be connected to. I remember walking through the baby section of the military exchange, feeling numb. While other expectant mothers cooed over tiny baby clothes, I was consumed by fear, wondering, *What am I going to do with a baby?* I was in a foreign country with one friend and was about to bring a life into the world. Even in those moments of despair, God's grace was quietly working. I didn't know it then, but He was already laying the foundation for something greater—through people, timing, and circumstances I never would have planned.

One thing I've learned about the Navy is that the word *Shipmate* carries weight—it means everything. We take care of our own. And one of those shipmates was already being positioned to be part of God's provision. He was the one who had convinced me to take those orders for the ship in the first place. I was adamant about not wanting to go overseas, but he kept urging me, saying, "Go. I'm coming right behind you." And sure enough, he did. When I knocked on his door to tell him I was pregnant, he didn't judge me, question me, or pull away—he gave me the biggest hug.

I broke down, sharing my fears and uncertainty, and he reassured me, saying, "You're going to be fine. We've got a nephew coming." In that moment, it felt like a weight lifted off my shoulders. That moment reminded me: even when you feel unprepared, unseen, or unsure, God will still send the right people at the right time to hold you up. For the first time, I began to believe that maybe, just maybe, everything would be okay. God is intentional about everything He does, especially when it comes to the people He places in our lives.

While I was in limbo waiting to report to my new duty station, I was placed in a holding company. The Security Officer, who I'd met during ship inspections, was in charge there. I called to ask if I could temporarily work in his office while my orders were being finalized, and without hesitation, he and his team welcomed me in with open arms.

After about two weeks in the office, the Security Officer invited me to church. Now, going to church wasn't new for me—I grew up attending Sunday school and services—but what I didn't expect was the surprise waiting for me when I arrived. I walked into the church, and I discovered that he was the Pastor. I was shocked. What started as a simple work connection turned into something far greater. That church became my family, surrounding me with love and support during one of the most challenging times of my life. God knew exactly what I needed before I even realized it myself. Even though I didn't have any family close by, my shipmates became my family. They rallied around me when I needed them most.

When I was about seven months pregnant, one of my shipmates, who was also a mom, came to me and asked if I was planning to have a baby shower. I remember responding sheepishly, admitting that at the beginning of my pregnancy, I had put a few baby items on layaway at the military exchange.

What I didn't say was how numb I had felt in those early months—so much so that I'd made the layaway to feel something, anything, when the time came to finally pay it off. She must have seen it on my face because she immediately said, *"Don't worry about it. I'll take care of it."* I was shocked by her generosity, but even then, I didn't think much of it. In my mind, I doubted anyone would even bother to show up. I wasn't sure if the relationships I'd built with my shipmates were strong enough to warrant that kind of support. The day of the baby shower changed everything for me.

I'll never forget walking into that room and seeing everyone. It felt like the whole world had come together just for me. They showered my soon to be little boy with so many gifts that I didn't have to buy a single thing for the first two years of his life. I'll never forget the day it all hit me. I was sitting alone, surrounded by baby items that had been gifted to me—diapers, tiny clothes, bottles, things I hadn't even thought to ask for. But it wasn't the stuff that overwhelmed me. It was the love behind it. The way people showed up. The beautiful way God moved through them. At that moment, I felt seen.

Not just as a soon-to-be mother, but as a woman who was scared, uncertain, and quietly wondering how she'd ever figure it all out. I had spent so much time trying to stay strong, trying to act like I had it under control—but deep down, I didn't. I was on the edge of a brand-new chapter, and everything in me felt unprepared. God wasn't surprised. He had already gone ahead of me, placing the right people in my life before I even knew I'd need them.

Just when I felt the most isolated and unsure, God reminded me of His promise: *"I will never leave you nor forsake you"* (Deuteronomy 31:6). Every detail, every act of kindness, every perfectly timed provision was His gentle way of saying, *"I see you. I got you. and You're never alone."*

He's not a bare-minimum God. He is the God of *exceedingly and abundantly more than we could ever ask or imagine.* It's in the humbling, vulnerable moments—when we finally admit, *"I don't have it all together"*—that His grace shines the brightest. That's where healing begins and the transformation happens. And for me? That's when love returned. Not the conditional kind I had known growing up—but real, redeeming, unconditional love. The kind that doesn't wait for you to have it all together. The kind that wraps you up, right in the middle of your mess, and says, *"You're still chosen."*

When we step into something new—becoming a parent, launching a product, starting a new job, or navigating a season where everything feels unfamiliar—it's easy to feel the pressure to have it all figured out. But in those moments, humility becomes our guiding light. It's not loud or flashy but rather a quiet confidence that whispers, *"If God called me here, He'll make a way."*

We see this so clearly in Esther's story. She didn't storm into the throne room demanding justice or making bold declarations. Instead, she invited King Xerxes and Haman to a banquet. And that banquet? It wasn't weakness—it was *warfare*. It was a calculated move led by discernment and was covered in prayer. She moved with intention, and wisdom. Esther understood that the outcome wasn't hers to orchestrate—it was God's to deliver. Her role was to prepare, position, and pray. God's role was to move hearts, expose truth, and protect His people. That was humility in action.

Esther was teaching us something powerful: you can confront the very thing that's trying to destroy you—with a level of meekness that screams boldness. That's the beauty of God-centered leadership—it doesn't always shout, and it never withdraws. Esther showed us that meekness isn't the absence of power—its power under control. And in the hands of a woman aligned with her assignment, that kind of bold humility can have global impact.

Humbling Ourselves to Embrace God's Plan

Our egos can be sneaky and sometimes have us slipping into a "me first" mentality without even noticing it. We start thinking it's our hustle alone that will get us where we want to go, or that we have to prove ourselves to everyone around us. But here's the truth, God can do way more in our lives when we step aside and let Him take the lead. The moment we humble ourselves, the possibilities for growth and impact open up in ways we never imagined.

If you've ever asked yourself, *What is my calling? How do I know if I'm walking in my assignment?* —you're not alone. We often think of purpose as this grand, crystal-clear aha moment. But more often than not, it's something much simpler.

The word *calling* comes from the Latin word *vocare* which means "to call." At its core, calling is really about God inviting us into something deeper—first into a relationship with Him, and then into a life that reflects His purpose for us. Over time, people started using the word *calling* to describe the different ways we live out our faith—whether that's through our work, our ministry, or just how we show up in the world.

I love how Dr. Scott Berthiaume, the president of Dallas International University, broke it down during a chapel talk. He explained that there are three parts to our calling. First, there's the call to faith—that's our foundation. Then, there's the call to a specific type of work or ministry—the thing we're uniquely gifted to do. And finally, there's the call to a particular context—the people, places, and spaces where God is asking us to serve.

That helped me so much, because sometimes we get stuck trying to figure out the *what and where*, but forget to check in with the *who*. And girl, when those three things line up? That's when purpose starts to click. That's when calling becomes more than a question—it becomes direction.

Three Ways to Identify Your Calling

1. What keeps pulling at your heart?

Your calling isn't always something new—it's often something you've been running from or overlooking. What problems burden you? What dreams, ideas, or themes keep resurfacing in your thoughts and conversations? Sometimes the thing that bothers you the *most*—even when others seem unbothered—is a sign of *divine agitation*. Divine agitation is often a clue that God is calling *you* to do something about it. What breaks your heart, frustrates your spirit, or keeps you up at night? Pay attention to what won't leave you alone—it may be heaven's nudge toward your assignment.

2. Where do you see the most fruit?

God has already equipped you with gifts that naturally serve others. What do people consistently come to you for? What do you do with ease that others find valuable? Often, our purpose is hidden in what we do so effortlessly that we take it for granted. What do people seek your advice on? Where do you make an impact with ease?

3. What requires faith?

Your assignment will often stretch you beyond your comfort zone.

Look at Esther, she didn't feel ready to lead, but she was positioned for it. If you feel unqualified, but you're in good company— that's often the exact place where God shows up and reveals His strength through your obedience.

The Role of Humility in Answering Your Call

Recognizing your calling isn't just about identifying what you're meant to do—it's about surrendering to God's plan for how to do it. When we approach our work, our dreams, and even our setbacks with this mindset, *Lord, You know best. Show me what steps to take,* we leave room

81

for God to move. Instead of forcing doors open, we allow Him to guide us to the ones He's already unlocked. We stop striving and start walking in divine alignment.

Pregnancy taught me some of the greatest lessons in humility. I remember vividly when God showed me that I was no longer in control. It was early on in my pregnancy. At the time, I thought I was doing a great job at hiding it. I wore loose-fitting clothes, watched what I ate and drank, and tried to carry on as though nothing had changed. One day, I went to a birthday party at a skating rink. It seemed like a fun break from my routine of just going to work and heading straight home.

When I tell you I had a time, girl—a time was had. I was laughing, singing, dancing, and even skating. For the first time in a long while, I didn't even feel pregnant. I felt free. Light. Almost like myself again. And then—*the cake.* A slice of white cake with ice cream, and baby, it was like I had never tasted cake before in my life. It was *so* good—one of the best things I'd had in a long time. Sweet, simple, and just what my soul needed. As the night wound down and I headed to my car, I smiled and thought, *Wow, I had such a great time. Look at me—see, I can do this. I can carry on like usual.*

At that moment, it felt like maybe everything would be okay.

Then—*out of nowhere*—I felt a strange sensation in my stomach. Before I could even process what was happening, I started vomiting— right there in the middle of the road. The closest thing to me was a drain, and the way it all came up had people around me genuinely concerned. I was mortified. Completely embarrassed. I got into my car and cried the entire way home. I collapsed on the bathroom floor on my knees, completely undone. The emotions I had been holding in, all the pretending, all the fear—finally spilled out in one breathless prayer:

"Okay, God. I get it. You're in control. I submit."

And I meant it. The very next day, I walked into the uniform shop and bought my first set of maternity uniforms. No more hiding. No more pretending. No more acting like I could carry on like nothing had changed.

It was in that moment of complete vulnerability—when I felt the most exposed and out of control—that I realized we can't hide from God. We can't outrun His will. And no matter how tightly we try to hold the reins, He will always lovingly lead us back to a position of surrender. What I thought was a setback—a loss of control—was actually a gift. It was God's gentle way of reminding me to stop running and to trust him regardless of the circumstances.

It's easy to want to show only the well-put-together version to the world—you know, the beautiful highlight reel playing to the perfect soundtrack. They don't see the breakdowns on bathroom floors, the whispered prayers through tears, or the moments when we felt completely stuck and unsure of what's next.

We've all had moments when we looked strong on the outside but were falling apart on the inside. And it's in *those* moments—the raw, real, unfiltered ones—where God shows up—not to shame us but to *shape* us.

Imagine if Esther had let her doubts stop her—if she'd decided not to go to the king because she thought she wouldn't be heard. How different would her story have been? The thing is, Esther didn't do it alone. She had Mordecai and her praying circle backing her up, and most importantly, she put her trust in God over her feelings. That's precisely how we have to approach those wilderness seasons in our lives. Everything changes when we're humble enough to see failures as lessons instead of personal defeats.

Suddenly, we're no longer throwing pity parties or sitting in frustration. Instead, we ask God, *"Okay, what do You want me to learn from this? How can I grow through this?"* But let me be clear: I'm not saying we won't ever wrestle with doubt. We're human. Even some of the most powerful people in the Bible questioned God and themselves. Abraham doubted he could ever be a father in his old age—yet God made him the father of many nations. Moses doubted his ability to lead and speak, asking how someone like him could stand before Pharaoh and deliver an entire nation. And yet, he was the one God chose to lead His people toward the Promised Land.

God isn't intimidated by our flaws—He uses them. He takes what feels like failure, insecurity, or hesitation and flips it completely. It's never really about our qualifications. It's about our *willingness*.

If humility positions us for purpose, then pride can push us completely out of alignment. Let's be clear: the opposite of humility isn't strength—it's arrogance. Pride is sneaky. It'll dress itself up as confidence, but in reality, it's a need to prove, control, or impress. It thrives in comparison, feeds on applause, and silently convinces you that you don't need anyone—not even God.

But here's what I've learned:

Pride protects image. Humility protects impact.

Pride says, *"I've got this."* Humility says, *"God, I trust You in this."*

When we rely solely on our strength, we become limited by our capacity. But when we walk in humility, we're led by God's strength—and there's no ceiling to what He can do through us.

It's knowing you're gifted, but also knowing those gifts came from God. It's recognizing your influence, while remembering that your influence is meant to serve, not to elevate your ego.

We see the danger of unchecked pride so clearly in the story of Esther—through the life of Haman. He had power, position, and access to the king. From the outside, it looked like he had it all. But it was never enough. One man—Mordecai—refusing to bow was all it took to unravel him. That's what pride does. It inflates our sense of self and distorts our ability to lead with clarity. Haman couldn't see past his own ego, and in trying to destroy someone else, he set the trap that ultimately destroyed *himself.*

And sis, the same is true for us. Pride doesn't always show up loud and obvious. Sometimes it sneaks in wearing confidence, but underneath—it's still pride.

Pride will always pull us toward performance, image, and self-reliance. It convinces us we have to prove something. That we have to earn love, secure validation, or control outcomes. But here's what pride can really look like:

- **Arrogance** – an inflated sense of self-importance or superiority
- **Entitlement** – believing you deserve something without earning it
- **Self-righteousness** – assuming you're morally or spiritually better than others
- **Unhealthy self-reliance** – trusting only in your own strength instead of God's

In a biblical context, pride is often the root of many downfalls.

Proverbs 16:18 reminds us:

> *"Pride goes before destruction, and a haughty spirit before a fall."*

Pride is a posture that closes us off—from growth, correction, and the voice of God. It hardens us. isolates us. and eventually, it can ruin the very thing we were called to build.

But humility does the opposite. Humility keeps us surrendered, soft, moldable, and ready. It invites God in. It says, "I don't have to have it all figured out. I just need to be led by the One who does." God isn't asking for perfection—He's asking for correct posture. When you're postured in humility, you're positioned for elevation.

Humility Beyond Leadership

Girl, let's take this conversation beyond business titles and leadership platforms for a minute. Humility doesn't just shape us into strong leaders, it makes us better spouses, partners, parents, and friends. When we're humble, we're more patient with our children. We stop seeing their behavior as personal attacks and start viewing every challenge as an opportunity—for *them* to grow and for *us* to mature alongside them. Humility softens our tone and opens our ears. It reminds us that we're not raising perfect kids—we're raising people who need grace, just like we do.

As partners and spouses, humility shifts the goal from *winning* the argument to *protecting* the relationship. It becomes less about being right and more about staying aligned. Humility shifts our perspective from "me vs. them" to "us—under God's guidance."

Here's the best part: when we lean into humility, we tap into God's limitless supply of the fruits of the spirit. We stop running on fumes and start operating from a place of overflow. Living with a humble heart reminds us that God doesn't make mistakes. Even when life doesn't match the blueprint we had in mind, His plan is never off track. His purpose for us is always greater than our expectations, and His rewards always outshine what we thought we wanted.

Our humility honors God more than any big speech, stage performance, or Instagram-worthy moment ever could. When we live by faith and trust His promises more than we chase our desires, we're showing Him that we believe His Word is more solid than our worries. That truth seeps into how we love, serve, and treat the people closest to us. Think about when Jesus took two loaves and a few fish and fed thousands. He didn't ask for a grand offering or demand a five-course feast. He just asked for what was willingly given.

If He can take something so simple and multiply it to feed a multitude, imagine what He can do with a heart that trusts Him—even with just a mustard seed of faith. On our own, our efforts might never feel like enough. We may look at our resources, time, and gifts—and think they're too small. But the moment we place them in God's hands, He multiplies them. He makes what we have more than enough. Now, let's be clear, being humble doesn't mean we see ourselves as inadequate or incapable. It's quite the opposite. It means we recognize a deeper truth: we were never meant to walk this journey *without* God.

Just as God walked with Adam in the Garden of Eden, He walks with us—calling us by name, inviting us into daily partnership with Him. When we stop trying to carry it all on our own and finally say, *"God, I know You've got this."* Suddenly, we shift from panic to peace, performance to presence, pressure to purpose.

That's the power of humility. It's choosing to decrease so that God can increase. It's not about shrinking back—it's about making room for God to be seen through you.

And if anyone embodied that kind of posture, it was King David.

Let's talk about him for a moment.

He's one of the people I turn to when I need a heart check—especially when I feel like God has shown me something *greater*, but the process to get there is stretching me in ways I didn't expect. I know this as a fact—before you ever step into the palace, God will often humble you in the field.

Imagine this: you're a teenager, minding your own business out in the fields, tending sheep, when out of nowhere, the prophet Samuel shows up at your house. He's there on divine assignment—to anoint the next king of Israel. But your own father doesn't even think to call you inside. David was not only overlooked and forgotten, but he was left out of the room while his brothers were paraded in front of the prophet one by one. And yet, God wasn't confused. Samuel looked at each of Jesse's sons and thought, *this must be the one.* But God kept saying, *No, not him.*

Finally, Samuel had to ask, *"Is there anyone else?* "That's when David was called in—the youngest, the shepherd boy, the one no one even considered. The one who wasn't invited to the table was the one God had chosen all along. Here's what I love about this part of David's story: God had in mind before he even entered the room. This was definitely a Jeremiah 29:11 moment. God had plans for David before David was even planning what to do next.

Even though David was anointed to be king, he didn't walk into the palace the next day and take the throne. He went right back to the fields. Back to the quiet place of tending sheep where no one was clapping—but God was still watching. Before God promotes you publicly, He refines you privately.

Can you imagine being told you're chosen by God for something huge—and then waiting years to see it happen? That's the part we don't talk about enough. The waiting, the training, the hidden season. David didn't demand a crown. He didn't try to force his way to the throne. He trusted God's timing and kept serving faithfully where he was. It must have felt so confusing, but God used that season of waiting to shape David's character. There was no fast pass to the crown—only a process that taught David about patience, faithfulness, and total dependence on God.

David's story reminds us that being set apart doesn't always mean being seen right away. In our own lives when God starts stirring things up to position us exactly where He wants us, He may reshuffle relationships, close doors we thought would stay open, or move us into unfamiliar territory that feels anything but comfortable. It's humbling—because it reminds us that we can't rely on borrowed strength or secondhand strategies.

Remember when David tried to wear Saul's armor and it didn't fit. It wasn't made for him. The same is true for us—we can't try to talk like someone else, hustle like someone else, or mimic someone else's calling. God didn't design you to be a copy. He created you to be a reflection of His creativity and purpose. From the very beginning, He stitched a piece of him into your identity—before you took your first breath. If He can take a shepherd boy who was forgotten by his own father and raise him up to lead a nation, girl, imagine what He can do with your life when you stay humble, obedient and ready.

There's a phrase we used to say in the military that still sticks with me: *"We stay ready, so we don't have to get ready.* "That's exactly what this season is about. It's about doing the inner work—staying ready in your heart, your mindset, and your spirit. When God calls your name, you don't want to be scrambling to catch up—you want to be *positioned.*

It's not about having all the answers or proving yourself—it's about having a heart of clay and a yielded spirit. Humility keeps you grounded when opportunities come and surrendered when the spotlight shines. It reminds you that the calling is never about status—it's about stewardship.

So, when that moment comes, you can walk into your assignment with humility and boldness—fully equipped, fully surrendered, and fully prepared. Not because you forced it or made it happen but because you let God shape you in private. Elevation without preparation can crush you—but when you've been processed in humility, you're not just ready for the door to open… You're ready to walk through it and thrive.

Embracing Esther Energy

Now let's tap into that Esther Energy and remember: We are connected to a royal priesthood. God has intentionally placed us in our families, businesses, and communities for a reason. The influence we carry isn't just for our own benefit—it's so we can be marketplace leaders, strategic advisors, and spirit-led consultants to those we love and lead. When we truly recognize this, we begin to move differently. We're not just checking boxes on to-do lists and chasing clients—

we're walking out a divine mandate, orchestrated by a God who designed our gifts with purpose and intention.

Sometimes we search high and low for love, validation, or praise—straining to prove our worth in our roles as moms, entrepreneurs, leaders. But when we stop striving and start seeking God first—especially in our moments of inadequacy—He meets us right there. He reminds us that our worth isn't tied to sales numbers, social media likes, or applause. Our worth is sealed by His promise. He sees every sacrifice we make—every late night, every silent prayer, and every quiet act of obedience. As moms and career women, it's so easy to slip into "do-it-yourself" mode. We hustle hard, chase opportunity after opportunity, trying to make it all happen in our own strength—only to end up burnt out and spiritually depleted.

God's blessings begin to flow the moment we release control. He's not asking us to have it all figured out. He's waiting for us to loosen our tight-fisted grip, to let Him lead. When we stop trying to carry everything ourselves and start learning how to ask for help, delegate with wisdom, lean into the community God has placed around us, then we begin to thrive.

Our assignments are greater than the titles. Esther didn't rise to influence just to wear a crown. She was placed in position to fulfill a greater purpose—to deliver her people in a defining moment. Sis, in the same way, your business isn't "just a side hustle." It's not just a way to bring in income. It's a platform for Kingdom impact. It's a place where your faith can shine, where your story can encourage others, and where your obedience can create legacy. To embrace your Esther Energy is to walk boldly in who you are in Christ. It means operating in the authority He's given you and trusting that—even if you feel unseen or unappreciated—God is working behind the scenes on your behalf.

Esther Energy Prayer for Humility

Father God,

Thank You for reminding me that true leadership begins with humility. You have called me, chosen me, and set me apart for such a time as this—not to seek my own glory, but to reflect Yours. Help me to lead with grace, wisdom, and a heart that stays surrendered to You. Strip away every ounce of pride, striving, and self-promotion within me. Remind me that it is You who elevates, You who opens doors, and You who orders my steps.

When I feel unseen, ground me in the truth that I am Your special possession. When I feel the urge to control the outcome, soften my heart to trust in Your plan. When I'm tempted to push ahead without You, pull me back into alignment with Your will.

May I always remember that humility is my superpower, obedience is my strategy, and grace is my covering. As I walk this path of purpose, may my life be a reflection of Your light and love, leaving a legacy of faith, impact, and abundant blessing.

In Jesus' name,

Amen.

Reflection Questions:

1. Where in your life have you been forgetting that you are chosen and set apart? How can you begin to lead with the confidence of someone who carries God's light, even in spaces where you feel overlooked or underestimated?

    1 Peter 2:9 (NIV)

    "But you are a chosen people, a royal priesthood, a holy nation, God's special possession, that you may declare the praises of him who called you out of darkness into his wonderful light."

2. What area of your leadership or daily life have you been trying to control or elevate on your own? How can you surrender that to God today and allow Him to lift you in His perfect timing?

James 4:10 (NIV)

> *"Humble yourselves before the Lord, and he will lift you up."*

3. Where do you feel uncertain or unclear about your next steps? How can you shift from relying on your own understanding to fully trusting God's direction and provision?

Proverbs 3:5-6 (NIV)

> *"Trust in the Lord with all your heart and lean not on your own understanding; in all your ways submit to him, and he will make your paths straight."*

ENDURE AND REFINE

"Blessed is the one who perseveres under trial because, having stood the test, that person will receive the crown of life that the Lord has promised to those who love him."

James 1:12 (NIV)

There's a season in every journey—whether in life, business, or faith—where everything feels still. No breakthroughs. No applause. Just silence. I call it the off-season—the space between preparation and promise, where endurance and resilience are tested the most. This is where many quit—right in the middle—assuming that silence means God has stepped away, or worse, that his plan is no longer in motion. Imagine if Esther had done the same. What if she had walked away after the banquet, celebrated exposing Haman, and thought the job was done? Seriously, what if she had mistaken exposure for completion, the breakthrough would've never manifested.

We can never let exposure or influence distract us from God's assignment. Just because the enemy is revealed doesn't mean the battle is over. We see this clearly in Esther's story. Haman was out of the picture—yes. And justice had begun, but the decree to annihilate the Jews hadn't been reversed. The system that enabled destruction was still in motion. The threat hadn't been fully dealt with—it had only been revealed. And that's the trap many of us fall into mistaking visibility for victory. When we experience a moment of clarity or insight, we often think we've "made it." It's easy to confuse being seen with being finished, but the real purpose doesn't stop at visibility. It finishes what God started. Exposure is often the invitation to keep pressing forward. It encourages us to lean in after the applause and stay focused on the assignment—because obedience isn't proven in the spotlight; it's solidified in the follow-through. Esther's follow-through required her to use her voice again. Her final plea wasn't for recognition, riches, or revenge—it was for something only the king could grant time. That moment wasn't marked by applause or public celebration. It was strategic. Esther and Mordecai were granted time to prepare the Jewish people to stand, to fight, and to survive. That decision, made in a quiet moment of courage, became the turning point. Sometimes, the greatest victories aren't won in front of the crowd—they're secured in the quiet places of strategy and obedience.

The off-season isn't just about waiting—it's about preparing wisely. It's where God works in the unseen, stretching your faith, shaping your character, and setting you up for a breakthrough that requires your obedience—not just your visibility.

Proverbs 21:31 (NIV) puts it perfectly: *"The horse is made ready for the day of battle, but victory rests with the Lord."*

This verse is a powerful reminder that while we trust God for the outcome, we still have a role in getting ready—spiritually, mentally, and strategically. Esther did her part. She didn't wait for deliverance to just fall into place—she acted in wisdom, positioned her people, and trusted that God would do the rest. We are called to do the same. This chapter is for women in the waiting season. The woman who feels stuck between vision and fulfillment. The leader that questions if she has the strength to keep going. To the mother who questions her worth and purpose. The off-season isn't a sign that you're forgotten—it's a sign that you're being fortified.

Your off-season is part of your training ground. It's in the quiet moments where your spiritual muscles are strengthened, your mindset is tested, and your identity is secured—not on the podium, but on the track where no one's watching.

In the world of track and field—where milliseconds define champions and setbacks can shatter dreams—there exists a story of resilience and redemption that goes far beyond the sport itself. Enter Sha'Carri Richardson. Her name is etched in the history books not just for her blazing speed, but for her unyielding spirit in the face of adversity. Her journey didn't follow the script of a smooth rise to greatness. Instead, it started with a setback so public, so crushing, that it could have ended her career before it truly began.

Now, if you don't know her story, girl . . . where have you been? No worries—I got you. Back in 2020, the world watched as Richardson's dreams of competing in the Tokyo Summer Olympics came to a screeching halt. A positive drug test ended her Olympic hopes. But this wasn't some scandalous downfall—it was pain, grief, and coping in real time. Leading up to that moment, she admitted to self-medicating with marijuana to deal with the sudden death of her birth mother. A loss so heavy, she did what many of us do when the weight of the world feels unbearable—she tried to numb the pain.

Rules are rules, and the World Anti-Doping Agency and USA Track & Field suspended her. Just like that, the opportunity she had worked for her entire life was snatched away. The 30-day ban was expected, but her name being left off the USA Olympic Team entirely? That was not. With gut-wrenching disappointment, Sha'Carri Richardson went on the Today Show to speak about the ban. She could have made excuses and shifted blame. And honestly? No one would have blamed her if she had. But instead, she took accountability.

"I know what I did. I know what I'm supposed to do . . . I still made that decision," she told the Today Show host. "Right now, I'm just putting all of my time and energy into dealing with what I need to do, which is to heal myself," That decision—to own her mistake instead of running from it—changed the trajectory of her life. Because, let's be real, we all have moments we wish we could do over. Decisions we regret. Delays we didn't expect. Setbacks that shook us to the core. Looking back, we realize that even those setbacks were shaping us into who we were meant to be.

For Richardson, that meant losing the biggest opportunity of her career while being constantly reminded of her choices by sports critics and headlines. Despite the negative press, the criticism, the world labeling her "finished," she refused to let that moment define her. Instead, she did what champions do. She took full responsibility, redirected her energy, and got to work. Here's the thing: Pain is heavy, but Purpose is heavier. Richardson wasn't just grieving her mother— she was grieving the weight of a public failure. Some headlines questioned her character; others mocked her reasons for breaking the rules.

While the world counted her out, she used the off-season as her proving ground. Every sprint. Every workout. She locked it. She let the whispers of doubt become fuel. And when the moment came to rewrite the narrative—she seized it. At the 2023 World Athletics Championships, Richardson stepped onto the track with lion-hearted confidence and determination. With every stride, she defied expectations, leaving her competitors in a trail of dust as she surged toward the finish line. She blazed past the competition in a breathtaking display of speed and skill, securing the victory in the 100-meter dash. She had become the world's fastest woman.

This wasn't just about a race. This was a visual representation of what it looks like to leave the past behind and push forword towards the goal. When Richardson crossed the finish line, the world erupted. During a post-race interview, when asked how it felt to be back, she responded with a phrase that would become a rallying cry for underdogs everywhere: "I'm not back. I'm better." And that's the lesson. Success isn't just about the spotlight—it's about the work that happens in the dark. True victory isn't just about winning—it's about healing. And setbacks aren't the end of the story. They are just God's way of pushing us to something greater.

Richardson flipped the script on adversity. And if she can do it? So can we. For Richardson, the road to success was paved with disappointments and challenges. Richardson's perseverance remained unshakable through every obstacle, propelling her toward her ultimate purpose. In the face of adversity, she emerged as a champion on the track and a beacon of hope and inspiration for all who dared to believe in do-overs.

Like athletes, we all go through an off-season—a time dedicated to preparation and refinement. It's during these seasons of rest, reflection, and realignment that we gain the strength and clarity needed to step fully into our God-given assignments.

It's where priorities shift, faith deepens, and our capacity is stretched. These moments may be quiet, even uncomfortable, but they are absolutely necessary. Operating in your purpose requires more than just talent and strategy—it demands divine endurance.

That's why Esther Energy isn't rooted in hustle culture—it's grounded in God's perfect timing. It's not about grinding to prove your worth—it's about aligning with the One who already called you worthy. When God positions you, you don't have to force what He's already favored. Like Esther, your journey will include hidden seasons, bold decisions, delayed answers, and a trust that's grounded in God—not outcomes.

Faith. Leadership. Intention. Persistence. (FLIP)

The FLIP Framework is designed to guide you through the tension that shows up when you decide to stop playing small and start flipping the script in your life. The goal isn't to survive your calling—it's to thrive in it, with God at the center. We live in a society that constantly shouts: *Put yourself first. Push harder. Power through. Heal yourself. Be your own savior.* We've bought into it.

We convince ourselves we can handle it all. We repeat mantras like, *"I will push through."* We tell ourselves, *"Fill your own cup first."*

But let's be real, sis—we're not strong enough, smart enough, or strategic enough to do this in our own power.

God already told us:

> *"For My thoughts are not your thoughts, neither are your ways My ways,"* declares the Lord. *"As the heavens are higher than the earth, so are My ways higher than your ways and My thoughts than your thoughts."*

— Isaiah 55:8–9

Even at our best, we still run dry. And it doesn't always happen all at once. First, it starts off subtle. You're a little more tired than usual. You're snapping at the people you love cause your stretch too thin. You're distracted in prayer—or avoiding it altogether and then it progresses into tightness in your chest that you keep calling "just stress." It's going through the motions while secretly wondering if any of it matters. It's drowning in anxiety. It's smiling in public and crying behind closed doors. It's depression that lingers like a cloud. It's the silent pressure to keep showing up when you feel completely empty inside. It's scrolling endlessly, not to connect—but to escape. It's overthinking every decision.

Before you know it, you're running on fumes—physically present but spiritually empty. That's what happens when we try to refill from sources that were never meant to sustain us. And sis, hear me—you're not alone. We've all been there. But this isn't just about getting your cup filled. It's about what's in your cup.

If we're being honest, some of us have been sipping on *jealousy, comparison, manipulation,* or *performative perfection*—and wondering why we feel so depleted. But we were never meant to refill ourselves with performance, pressure, or hustle. We were meant to be refilled by God—The One who restores, renews, and refreshes us from inside out. Because whatever's in your cup is what you'll pour out.

99

So, if you're filled with anxiety, bitterness, or insecurity—that's exactly what shows up in your leadership, your family, your decisions, and your relationships. But when God is your source—when you're filled with wisdom, grace, and love—you're not operating from lack. You're pouring from a place of *overflow*.

And that's what this whole framework is about. It's about shifting from uncertainty to clarity, from fear to dominion, from waiting to boldly walking into your assignment—fully confident that the same God who called you is the One who will carry you.

He said,

"I will be with you wherever you go."

— **Joshua 1:9**

And He meant it. Just as He was with those in the Bible—just as He was with Jesus in His final breath—He is with you right now. Pause and let that settle. We often believe God is near when everything is going right, when doors are opening, and when the favor is flowing. But He is just as present in our lowest, quietest, and most uncertain moments. He is unchanging. The same God who told Joshua, *"Just as I was with Moses, I will also be with you,"* is the same God who walks with us today.

He hasn't forgotten you.
He's not distant.
He's not waiting on you to get it all together.

He seeks after us as we seek Him, directing, guiding, orchestrating, protecting, healing, blessing, and comforting us through every season. We must be reminded: Our purpose is not just about personal success; it's about being living proof that God is still the God of miracles. It's about aligning with His will, trusting His timing, and showing up fully prepared when your moment arrives—so that when it happens, no one can call it luck. Instead, it will be undeniable divine orchestration by the Most High, living God. It takes purpose to live aligned with purpose.

I remember sitting at my desk, doom-scrolling on Instagram while half-listening to the playback of a hot seat coaching call. I was distracted—mentally tired, emotionally drained, and caught in the cycle of comparison without even realizing it.

Then a question in the chat caught my attention:

"How do I set boundaries with social media posting for my business? I keep getting caught in the rabbit hole of scrolling."

The coach's response was simple, but it hit me like a ton of bricks:

"As a multi-millionaire, I don't have time to scroll. Social media is a tool. I am a disruptor, a creator—not a consumer."

She went on to explain how she didn't even have the app on her phone. She only posted on social media from her laptop. She went on further and explained how she had mastered the strategy of going viral by studying her audience—learning what they needed, and building offers that solve real problems. She was intentional, focused, and purpose driven. And something in her response shifted something in me.

It wasn't just about productivity—it was about stewardship. After that call, I made a bold decision: I went on social media fast.

What started as 30 days turned into 40. I texted my prayer partner about it, and she called me immediately to pray. She already knew what was coming. She knew the attacks would hit my mind, my identity, and my discipline.

Now, let me tell you why I went on that fast. I got tired of playing God. I was stuck in a cycle of comparison—setting goals that looked good on paper but weren't rooted in obedience to what God was actually calling me to do.

They were rooted in impressing people. I had gotten to a point where I couldn't even hear God's voice—because it was buried under all the noise I was consuming.

Here's the thing: God created us in His image to be creators, not consumers. But somewhere along the way, I let the scroll replace my surrender. I was hustling hard, praying for creativity, discipline, and focus—while completely neglecting the stewardship of what He had *already* given me. My focus wasn't fueled by obedience. It was driven by outcomes, metrics, and validation.

So, I decided to flip the script. I reframed my thinking and my actions. I put a system in place—one that put God first. I got intentional about what I was consuming—not just visually, but spiritually, emotionally, and physically.

The results were life changing. I became more productive in my home and my business. I started creating with purpose, not pressure. I started to hear God's voice more clearly than ever before. And let's just say—even the scale started moving. When you stop feeding your mind junk, you start making better choices in every area of your life—including your health. Turns out, the clarity I was praying for didn't come from doing more—it came from consuming less and surrendering more.

When you realign with God, everything shifts. Now, I'm not saying you have to go on social media fast—but the first step in flipping your life is getting into a posture where you can truly hear from God. In the Bible, fasting and prayer have always been ways to draw near to God for clarity, wisdom, and direction.

So, ask yourself honestly:

What's standing in the way of me hearing God more clearly?

What am I over consuming?

Proverbs 23:2 warns us about gluttony, a form of greed—typically associated with food, but it applies to so much more. In reality, we can consume too much of anything—social media, entertainment, validation, even work. And when we over consume, we unknowingly open the door to sin. How? Because when we constantly fill ourselves with the world, we begin to covet what others have instead of trusting what God has for us.

That's when comparison creeps in, jealousy stirs, and we lose sight of our purpose. Maybe for you, it's not social media.

Maybe it's gossiping.
Maybe it's negative self-talk.
Maybe it's self-doubt or self-sabotage—constantly questioning yourself instead of trusting God's plan.

Here is a reflection point:

What am I feeding my mind and spirit daily?
Am I spending more time scrolling than seeking?
Am I filling my life with distractions instead of God's direction?
Whatever it is—surrender it and have faith that God will create in you, new habits and mindsets. That's where it all begins.

Which brings us to the first part of the FLIP framework: Faith.

F – Faith

Esther didn't know how things would turn out when approaching the king. She didn't have a five-step plan or a confirmation that everything would go her way. The only thing she knew was she needed to have faith in God.

And that's what *faith* is. It's not about having all the answers. or waiting until you feel completely ready. It's about walking boldly, even before you can see the outcome. Faith fuels boldness and boldness rooted in God's word leads to destiny. One of the hardest seasons to be in is the one where the path isn't clear, the next step feels too risky, and the outcome is unknown. That uncomfortable, uncertain space is also one of the most beautiful places to be in because that's the space where you learn what it means to fully depend on God.

Not your title.
Not your strategy.
Not your followers, your finances, or your feelings.
Just Him.

It's where God becomes more than a backup plan. He becomes your source, your strength, and your strategy.

Faith: Trusting God Even When the Path Isn't Clear

Remaining close to God isn't just a good idea during uncertainty—it's necessary. The closer you are to Him, the clearer His direction becomes. Look at Abraham in Genesis 22:12-13, God told him to sacrifice Isaac—his promised son—and he obeyed.

Even when Isaac asked, *"Where's the lamb for the offering?"* Abraham answered by faith: "God will provide.

He took his son, tied him up, laid him on an altar he built for God, and reached for the knife to slay him. And just as he was about to do it—God called out:

"Don't lay a hand on the boy. There's a ram in the bush. "God said, *"Now I know that you love me because you were willing to sacrifice your only son.* "That's next-level obedience. Now imagine if he had only obeyed the *last* thing God said… and never checked back in. To be honest, that's how a lot of us move. We get one word from God and run with it—but we aren't close enough to discern when the plan shifts. Or we have faith to believe the vision but struggle to have faith to act on it in obedience. Abraham didn't wait for all the details. God gave him one word—and he moved.

No overthinking.
No bargaining.
No stalling.
Just obedience.

104

That's why he's called the Father of Faith, but if it were up to me, I'd call him Abraham About That Action—because he was ready to move! The truth is, one word from God isn't always enough to carry us forever. We must go back to Him daily, we need fresh instructions, renewed strength, and spiritual clarity.

You can't keep running on yesterday's word like it's still today's assignment. That's why Jesus taught us to pray: " *Give us this day our daily bread.*" — *Matthew 6:11* Because we need a *fresh word*—not spiritual leftovers. God reminds us in His Word:

> *"Man shall not live by bread alone, but by every word that proceeds from the mouth of God."*

> **— Matthew 4:4**

That means staying spiritually connected, checking in, and listening again to make sure we're aligned with His latest instructions just like Esther.

Her journey wasn't one of certainty, but of courage. She had to move forward despite the unknown, trusting that she was truly created for such a time as this—believing that God had positioned her purpose. Now, let's take a moment and put ourselves in her shoes. The man she regarded as a father figure was in deep distress. Her entire lineage was on the verge of being wiped out—by a decree given by the same man who had chosen her to be Queen. Imagine the emotions she must have felt. The weight of it, the fear and the pressure after just stepping into her royal position. She was faced with a decision that could cost her everything.

In moments like this, the easier option is to run—just like the Israelites wanted to do when they saw the Red Sea standing in their way. Instead of moving forward in faith, they cried out, wishing they had stayed in Egypt. They were ready to retreat, to go back to bondage because the unknown seemed too risky. But Esther's obedience opened the door for God's favor. And we see it in the king's response.

The moment he saw Esther, he was so pleased with her that he was willing to give her anything she asked for.

That is how God is with us. When we choose to stop running, when we stand in obedience and faith, when we fast, pray, and seek Him—God moves on our behalf. He opens doors we could never open on our own. He makes the impossible possible. So, the next time fear tells you to run, remember this: God didn't bring you this far to leave you. Just like He parted the sea for the Israelites and made way for Esther, He will bring you through, too. But first, you must have the faith to step forward.

Many of us find ourselves in similar situations—called to step into roles, opportunities, or seasons that feel intimidating or like we are not qualified. But just as Esther was prepared for her moment, we, too, are being prepared. The waiting, the refining, the hidden seasons—all of it is shaping us for the assignment ahead. To embody Esther Energy means to embrace the unknown with faith, to trust in God's divine orchestration, and to take action with wisdom and boldness. In these moments of surrender, we experience the fullness of God's power, walking in purpose with confidence, knowing that He goes before us. Faith will take you down a path that shows you how God not only hears your prayers but also never forgets.

Ever since I was a little girl, I had one prayer for my mother. Even though I didn't know where she was in the world, I always prayed that God would protect her and, if she had to die, that it would be a peaceful death. At 19 years old, during my first duty station in Hawaii, I received a call from my brother that would shake me to my core. *"I found Mom."* I froze. Speechless. I literally couldn't form words. I stammered, *"What, where?"*

At that point, I didn't even know if she was alive. So, hearing those words—I found Mom—felt like stepping into an alternate reality. And then, I heard her voice. She said my name so casually, like we had just spoken yesterday. I had no idea what to say. What do you say to someone who has been gone almost your entire life? The only words I could manage were: *"Where have you been?"*

My brother told me he was riding through the streets of Atlanta when he saw her sitting outside a store in a shopping center. She never answered my question. She just said, *"I'm alright."* That was it. It would be another four years before I saw my mother in person.

At 23 years old, I saw my mother for the first time—and we spent Thanksgiving together, just me, her, and my brother. Sis, my heart was overflowing with joy, I don't even know if I had words for that moment before it happened, but when it did? It felt like the place where I felt like I fit. By then, my mother had been in recovery from alcoholism and was working at a church that did outreach for the unhoused. I remember driving through the streets of Atlanta with her—the same streets I once wandered as a little girl searching for her. It's crazy how time can shift everything.

I can still see that version of me, walking to the neighborhood pool hall, hoping I'd find her inside. You would've thought I was a teenager the way I moved, but I wasn't. I was just a little girl. I always wondered what made my mom stop drinking. What was the turning point? The moment everything shifted for her. So, on the ride back to her place, I finally asked, **"Mama, what made you stop drinking?"** She paused for a moment, looked ahead, then quietly said something that would stay with me forever:

"God wouldn't allow me to get drunk anymore.

She told me that no matter how much liquor she drank, she just couldn't get drunk—as if God had taken it away Himself. That was when I realized that even when we run and drown ourselves in coping mechanisms, addictions, and self- destruction, He still pursues us. God has the power to break every chain. He wasn't just after her sobriety—He was after her soul. When I was a teenager, my aunt—who raised me—told me, *"Never let your mother's decisions be an excuse for your life."*

At the time, it felt like tough love but now I understand that it was her way of motivating me to rise above my circumstances, no matter where I started. We all have a starting point, and for years, I didn't even know what my mother's starting point was in Atlanta. It was a question that lingered in my mind, but I didn't have the answers. Then, one day, my aunt finally shared the story with me.

She grew up in a small town in Clairton, Pennsylvania. My grandmother had seven children—two were twins who passed away at birth, and my mom was the sixth of seven kids. As a teenager, my mother and some friends attempted to prank a man—but the prank went terribly wrong. The man was severely injured —so badly they thought he was dead. And just like that, my mother went on the run. She left behind my older brother—a baby at the time—with my grandmother and aunt. She fled to Atlanta, hoping to start over, to outrun the shame and consequences. To disappear into a new beginning.

Everyone has something they're running from. A mistake. A memory. A moment we wish we could erase. But some things you just can't outrun. No matter how far we go, God goes farther. Not to punish us but to redeem us. He doesn't chase us with a wrath—He pursues us with mercy.

Growing up in Atlanta was no fairytale. I wish I could say it was easy, but it wasn't. There were times when I experienced a normal childhood, but I was constantly reminded that I was just a little Black girl in Georgia in the 1980s. I still remember one beautiful day —the sun shining on my brown skin as I picked dandelions. I closed my eyes to make a wish and when I opened my eyes a white little boy had thrown a rock at me, and it hit me in the eye. I wanted to run home and tell someone but there was no one to run to.

Other memories are darker—literally. Oftentimes I was locked in from the outside—trapped in complete darkness, urinating in pickle jars, wondering if anyone would ever come for me. I had survived a childhood of instability—foster care, emotional abuse, and even some physical abuse—but nothing could have prepared me for this moment.

This time, it was my brother calling me again. *"You need to come home. It's Mom. She's in the hospital. It's not looking good."* I asked my brother to send a Red Cross message to my military duty station since it was such short notice. Within 24 hours, I was heading to my birthplace with my husband. I can't even put into words what I felt. All I knew was this: *Not going wasn't an option. It* was time to come face to face with some fears I had carried for years. The flight went by in a blur, but emotionally, it dragged on. I was on the verge of exploding with everything I had been holding in. Sleep was impossible—I tossed, turned, prayed, stared out the window the entire time.

When we landed, we went straight to the hospital. I didn't know what I was walking into. Before we walked in, my husband gave me a moment to breathe. There I was—sitting in the parking lot of the very hospital where the woman who gave me life…was now lying in a hospital bed, dying. I sat trying to remember the last time I spoke to my mother. It was during my wedding planning. I was in a local boutique, searching for an outfit for my bachelorette party, when the phone rang. *"Hey, Mom… what's up?"*

"I was calling to ask if I could walk you down the aisle." In a soft tone, I replied, well, Mom, I was going to have Uncle Sammy do it—since he's been like a father figure in my life. But I would love for you to be in the front row. Do you need me to buy your plane ticket?" In a split second, her voice went from sweet to sour. All I heard was "F-you, F-your husband." Click. Dial tone.

I was in complete shock. What just happened. Most women getting married would be asking their moms about the wedding colors or getting dress ideas, but no; instead, I sat on the other end of the phone listening to my mother screaming, "F- you!" And looking back now, isn't it ironic? People either reconnect at a wedding or a funeral.

Now, I was sitting outside the same hospital I was born in, listening to my aunt—who had been the mother figure in my life—asking me questions about a woman I barely knew. The questions came at me like darts: *"What are they going to dress her in? How is her hair? Does she have insurance? Are they going to put her in slippers?"*

Those questions smothered every other thought I had. *"So... are they going to dress her up in a gown?* " I don't know," I mumbled.

But deep down, I was burning with anger. One question kept gnawing at me, louder than all the rest: Why wasn't the woman who raised me here? This was her baby sister. Her blood. And yet, she wasn't sitting next to me. Never mind the fact that the person lying inside—was a woman I knew nothing about.

Simple things every child should know about their mother—felt like mysteries to me.

Her favorite color.
Her favorite perfume.
Her favorite food.
Her favorite TV show. I knew none of it.

My brother—someone I hadn't had a close relationship with for years—sat me down. His voice was heavy; his words slow and deliberate. "*I didn't want to tell you this over the phone.*"

I studied his face, trying to see how time had changed him. We once lived under the same roof briefly as kids, both staying with our aunt. But life, as it often does, pulled us in different directions. Still, he was my brother, and I held onto that. I still remember being a little girl, watching him walk through the door with giant teddy bears and balloons for my birthday. Those moments—simple as they were—felt like someone had remembered me.

When he got his own place, I would spend the weekends with him and his girlfriend. Cleveland felt like a world away from Georgia. I lived in the suburbs, had my own room, and had neighborhood friends to play with. For a little while, it felt like a normal childhood, but behind the scenes, things were happening that I wouldn't understand. One of those things was the selling of drugs. I was too young to see it, but my aunt saw everything. She accused my brother of living a lifestyle that could eventually bring harm to me. And so, just like that—she cut off all communication between us.

Then, one night, I sat in front of the television, tears streaming down my face as I watched the local news. There he was—my brother—being arrested outside the same neighborhood store I used to stop by after school. Another person was being taken away from my already fragile world.

We came from the same womb and shared similar childhood pain, but our journeys took very different paths. My brother spent eight years in prison, while I joined the Navy. Two paths, one blood. We wouldn't reconnect until after my first year in the Navy.

Now we were face to face, in a cold room, feeling just as empty as the space around us...Then, he said it. *"Mom is dying . . . She has AIDS and lung cancer."* The years of drinking, partying, and survival on the streets had taken a toll on her body. I sat there, numb. Processing. I don't think I even cried. He said, *"I'm going to take you in to see her while she is alert."*

When I walked into that hospital room and saw her—hooked up to a breathing machine, IVs in both arms—I didn't see the years lost or the pain endured. I just saw her. My mother who gave me life. I leaned in close, my voice barely above a whisper. "I'm here, Mama." The vital machines started going off and she attempted to communicate. Even though she was medicated, she knew who I was. I guess a mother always knows her child. I reached out and stroked her hair, just like I used to do when I was a little girl. And then—I did what I had always done. I prayed for her. But this time, my prayer was different. It wasn't, *"Lord, protect my mother."* It wasn't, *"And if she has to die, don't let her die a horrible death."*

No—this prayer was one of gratitude. A prayer of forgiveness. Because the truth is—God used her to bring me into this world. And even after all those years—He still heard my prayers. She passed away peacefully. Prayers answered, and he let me be there to be a witness. The place where I took my first breath is the place where the one who gave me life took her last breath. From that moment on, my brother vowed that nothing would ever come between us again. We were all we had left. Even though I had never heard her say, "I love you"— God's love covered me anyway.

When I was a child, I spoke as a child, and I reasoned as a child. I never had the capacity to understand her struggles as a woman and mother. The trauma-filled version of me had left Atlanta years ago. But that day? After I released it to God, the healed, inner little girl walked out of that room.

I share this story as a reminder that God hears your prayers— even the ones you whisper as a child. He doesn't forget them. He answers them at the appointed time. Every tear cried is stored up for joy. God took me back to the place where my journey began—the very hospital where I took my first breath. At first, it felt like a cruel twist of fate, but then I realized—it was never about the ending, it was about the full-circle of redemption. God was showing me that nothing is wasted. Not the pain, not the unanswered questions, not even the years of absence. He was showing me that He had been there all along, weaving my story together, bringing me back not just to my birthplace, but to a place of closure, healing, and undeniable faithfulness.

What started as brokenness was now a testimony of grace. What felt like abandonment was always His divine orchestration. Faith is trusting God when the story doesn't make sense, when the prayers feel unanswered, when the journey is painful.

God never left me, and He won't leave you either. Even when you can't see it, He is working. Even when it hurts, He is healing. Even when the path is unclear, He is leading. Trust Him. Step forward. Your faith is the key to the favor waiting on the other side. Like Esther, commit to prayer and fasting when seeking direction. Esther 4:16 reminds us that before she made her bold move, she fasted and prayed for three days—fully surrendering her situation to God before stepping forward in courage. Now it's your turn to take action, grab your journal.

1. Set a Time for Prayer & Fasting

Dedicate intentional time to seek God. Whether it's one day, three days, or more, commit to drawing closer to Him. Let this be a time of spiritual clarity and renewal.

2. Journal & Seek God

Document what God reveals to you during this time. Write down scriptures, insights, and confirmations. Keep your heart open— He may speak through His Word, a sermon, a conversation, or even a still small voice.

3. Track How God Shows Up

Keep record of the doors He opens, the wisdom He gives, and the shifts that happen in your life. Too often, we pray for something, receive it, and forget that it was God who made it happen. Writing it down allows you to look back and see His faithfulness in action.

4. Start Each Day with a Faith-Filled Affirmation

Speak life over your situation. Declare that God is working on your behalf and equipping you for your moment of favor.

Remember: Your faith activates the supernatural favor.

Leadership: Assigned, Aligned, and Anointed

If you've ever worn a uniform, clocked into a job, or sat in the pews on a Sunday morning, then you already understand the power of standards. And in the military? Baby, they don't play about them. There's a standard—and it's non-negotiable. You don't get to wake up and decide whether or not you *feel like* being excellent. There's an entire manual, a system, and expectations stacked on top of expectations. As a senior-level leader, your role isn't just about meeting the standard—it's about setting the tone for everyone around you.

That's exactly what Jesus did. He didn't roll deep with the disciples for clout or convenience. He *called* them, then taught them and corrected them all while earning their trust. And even still He didn't make a single move without consulting the Father. Wise counsel wasn't an afterthought—it was His lifestyle.

So as much as we love our vision boards and five-year plans, here's some real questions:

Are we setting the standard in our homes?

Are we setting the tone in our businesses?

Are we leading our teams with the same level of intention that Jesus did?

When you are assigned by God, aligned with His will, and anointed to lead, you don't have to force your way forward.

When you honor your authority, you uphold the standard, and you walk in confidence, knowing that God Himself has already endorsed your position.

L – Leadership

Leadership isn't one-size-fits-all. Just like we each have different callings, we also lead in different ways. Some are called to cast vision, while others are called to nurture growth. Some lead from the front,

114

while others lead from behind the scenes. The key is not to copy someone else's style—it's to understand your own, refine it, and make sure it aligns with God's assignment on your life.

Leadership isn't about fitting into a mold—it's about understanding how God uniquely designed you to lead. Whether you lead in the boardroom, the breakroom, or your own living room, the way you lead matters. Your leadership style can either build trust, create transformation, or hold people hostage to fear and confusion. That's why self-awareness is so powerful—it gives you the ability to lead with clarity, not just charisma.

In this next section, we're going to explore 7 common leadership styles. Each one has its own strengths, blind spots, and biblical parallels. You may find yourself in one—or you might be a blend of two or three. The goal here isn't to label you. The goal is to equip you to lead with more intention, alignment, and grace.

Let's Discover Your Leadership Style

1. Servant Leadership

Key Trait: Puts the needs of others first.

Example: Jesus washing the disciples' feet.

How it shows up: This leader empowers, listens, uplifts, and serves without needing the spotlight.

Faith style: This is Kingdom leadership—humility before authority.

2. Transformational Leadership

Key Trait: Inspires change and vision.

Example: Esther risking her life for her people.

How it shows up: Casts vision, raises the standard, and rallies others to grow beyond limitations.

Faith Style: Fueled by purpose and willing to sacrifice comfort for breakthrough.

3. Authoritative Leadership

Key Trait: Sets clear direction and expectations.

Example: Moses leading the Israelites with God-given instruction.

How it shows up: Clear, confident, directive—can be empowering *or* controlling depending on heart posture.

Faith style: Requires discernment—lead by revelation, not domination.

4. Democratic Leadership (Collaborative)

Key Trait: Values input and consensus.

Example: Nehemiah rebuilding the wall—delegating and gathering community.

How it shows up: Inclusive, team-oriented, often leads through collaboration and shared responsibility.

Faith style: Reflects the body of Christ—*many parts, one body.*

5. Laissez-Faire Leadership

Key Trait: Hands-off, minimal guidance.

Example: Can be necessary with strong, self-directed teams—but risky without accountability.

How it shows up: Freedom-heavy leadership.

Faith style: Can be wise if led by the Spirit and not fear of confrontation or laziness.

6. Transactional Leadership

Key Trait: Focuses on rules, tasks, and rewards/punishments.

Example: Think military structure—follow the system, get the reward.

How it shows up: Results-driven, efficient, but may lack emotional intelligence.

Faith style: Useful in structure but must be balanced with *grace and relationship*.

7. Coaching Leadership

Key Trait: Develops people's strengths and skills.

Example: Paul mentoring Timothy.

How it shows up: One-on-one investment, growth-centered, and nurturing.

Faith style: Reflects *discipleship*—investing in others for long-term impact.

When you combine your spiritual gifts with your natural strengths, that's where the oil flows—where leadership becomes not just a role, but a calling. Below are a few powerful tools you can use to discover and develop your unique leadership DNA:

Spiritual Gift Assessments

These help you uncover the gifts God has placed in you for Kingdom impact.

- **Spiritual Gifts Test**: www.spiritualgiftstest.com
Church Growth Spiritual Gifts Survey: www.giftstest.com

Natural Gifts & Leadership Style Assessments

These help you understand your personality, work style, and how you naturally lead or respond to challenges.

- **DISC Personality Assessment**: www.123test.com/disc-personality-test
- **Clifton Strengths (formerly StrengthsFinder)**: www.gallup.com/cliftonstrengths

Listen, I will never forget the day I was selected for Chief Petty Officer in the Navy. At the time, I was stationed at an Expeditionary Command in Dam Neck, Virginia—which, let me tell you, was a whole new world for me. Can I keep it real? The Admin Office there was already its own little reality show. The Chief had his favorites, and it was obvious. But honestly? That didn't bother me — not one bit. I wasn't there to collect friendship bracelets.

I was on a mission to pass my Chief's exam—period. My first go-round with the exam was the year before when I was stationed at the Pentagon. You had to be there by 7:30 a.m. with your ID card in hand—no excuses. I was pregnant, distracted, hungry, and unprepared. The short story? I failed. But that failure stayed with me—not as a source of shame, but as fuel. I made myself a promise that day: Never again will I show up unprepared.

While everybody else was grabbing lunch, hitting the gym, or chilling—I was posted up with my study guide, headphones in, fully focused. When the test results dropped and I read the word: Passed—it was game time.

Passing the exam was just the first step.

After that, it was time to submit my package to the board.

And listen, this wasn't one of those "click the link and get an instant answer" situations. No, ma'am. This was hurry-up-and-wait on a whole new level. When the day came it felt surreal. The whole command was buzzing because word had come down—Chief Petty Officer selection results would be released before noon.

I remember being so nervous. So, what did I do? I did what any reasonable human with anxiety and a little bit of sense would do:

I hid in the bathroom. Two knocks at the door. It was my career counselor. She cracked the door open and said, *"Is Chief Select Leftridge in here?"*

"BABY!" I screamed and ran down that hallway like my life depended on it. In that moment, everything changed. My title shifted from Petty Officer First Class to Chief Petty Officer (Select). Just like that, the celebration was over before it could even start. We had to be in the conference room by 3 p.m.—sharp.

Here's the part I loved the most: When you make Chief, they assign you a sponsor. Someone who's been where you're about to go. They guide you, challenge you, and make sure you don't just wear the anchors—you *carry them.*

Now, this isn't just some random person. Your sponsor becomes your lifeline. They encourage you, mentor you, hold you accountable. You cry to them, vent to them, and trust them as you go through the process. They are there to make sure you don't just wear the title but that you become the leader the title requires. This reminds me of Jesus and the disciples.

When He called them, they weren't sitting around waiting to be picked—they were already working and moving in purpose. Jesus didn't say, "Figure it out first." He said, *"Follow me."* And in that moment, not only did He call them—but He also renamed them. He redefined their identity and set a new standard: *"This is what it looks like to walk with me. Stay close, and I'll show you."*

That's the thing about elevation—it comes with expectation. You can't take the old you to the new level. The hardest part of growing is letting go of the person you used to be. The comfort zone, the habits, the mindset, and the version of yourself that was good enough back then but can't come with you into the new.

Esther showed us exactly what elevation looks like. Before she was Queen Esther, she was Hadassah. What started as just another girl entering a beauty pageant turned into her stepping into purpose—as the Queen of Persia. But make no mistake: it was never about the crown or the title. It was always about the assignment.

Here's what I need you to remember:

The world may know you by the name your parents gave you—but they don't know you by the name connected to your calling. When God promotes you—when He elevates you—it's not just about visibility. It's about anointing, the influence He's entrusting you with and the people tied to your obedience.

Sis, when you finally step into that new name, that new level, that new title— everything shifts.

So, if you're feeling the pull to something greater, lean into it.

Study.
Prepare.
Pray.
Stay ready.

One day, someone's going to knock on your metaphorical door and I hope—no, I pray—you throw your hands up, scream with excitement, and run toward that hallway of destiny with no fear, no hesitation, just obedience wrapped in joy.

When you walk in your God given assignment with intentionality, you stop operating like some secret agent, hiding your gifts, downplaying your purpose, and tucking away your anointing to make other people comfortable. You step fully into servant leadership. When you're on assignment from God, it's not about being seen, it's about serving well. It's about showing up with integrity, with humility, with love—knowing that every role you play, every room you enter, and every person you interact with is part of something so much bigger than you.

Jesus wasn't low-key about His purpose. He didn't stay tucked away in the shadows, hoping no one noticed the miracles. Nah, He led with audacity, loved openly, and still knew exactly when to pull away and pray. He knew how to teach in a way that didn't just reach people's minds but gripped their hearts. He understood the power of quiet devotion, those sacred moments when it was just Him and the Father. And no matter who misunderstood Him, doubted Him, or came against Him, Jesus stayed locked in. He knew why He was sent and he wasn't about to let anybody's opinions or intentions distract Him from it. He was the definition of purpose in motion.

Every step, every word, every miracle all aligned with God's perfect will. And if Jesus set the tone like that, what makes us think we're supposed to play it small or second-guess our calling? We must follow His lead. We must move with that same audacity. Remember when God assigns you, He also aligns you, and He most definitely anoints you for the position. You don't have to force it or fake it, you just need to believe it.

Esther stepped into leadership not by accident, but by alignment. She leaned into wise counsel, honored protocol, and created space for God to move. Together, she and Mordecai led their people not just with courage—but with strategy that shifted history.

This is your reminder: Servant leadership isn't just about boldness—it's about discernment, timing, and collaboration. Sometimes, God will give you the vision, but you'll need the right people beside you to carry it out. The plan may come from Him, but the execution often requires partnership. Now it's your time to uphold the standard and shift rooms when you walk it.

Activate Your Leadership

Here's your "Esther Energy Declaration" with scripture references to stand on as you speak life over yourself daily:

"I Decree & Declare":

I am chosen.

> *"You did not choose me, but I chose you and appointed you so that you might go and bear fruit—fruit that will last"* (John 15:16).

I am called.

> *"He has saved us and called us to a holy life—not because of anything we have done but because of his own purpose and grace"* (2 Timothy 1:9).

I am equipped.

> *"Equip you with everything good for doing his will, and may he work in us what is pleasing to him, through Jesus Christ, to whom be glory for ever and ever"* (Hebrews 13:21).

I release the old version of me and boldly step into the woman God created me to be.

> *"Therefore, if anyone is in Christ, the new creation has come: The old has gone, the new is here!"* (2 Corinthians 5:17).

I am ready to stop playing small to walking fully in my divine assignment.

> *"For we are God's masterpiece. He has created us anew in Christ Jesus, so we can do the good things he planned for us long ago"* (Ephesians 2:10).

I lead with grace.

"Let your conversation be always full of grace, seasoned with salt, so that you may know how to answer everyone" (Colossians 4:6).

I serve with love. Serve one another humbly in love" (Galatians 5:13).

I operate with excellence.

"Whatever you do, work at it with all your heart, as working for the Lord, not for human masters" (Colossians 3:23).

I am not here by accident.

"Before I formed you in the womb I knew you, before you were born I set you apart" (Jeremiah 1:5).

I am not here for applause or validation.

"Am I now trying to win the approval of human beings, or of God? Or am I trying to please people? If I were still trying to please people, I would not be a servant of Christ" (Galatians 1:10).

I am here on purpose, for purpose, with purpose.

"And we know that in all things God works for the good of those who love him, who have been called according to his purpose" (Romans 8:28).

The standard is set.

"But just as he who called you is holy, so be holy in all you do" (1 Peter 1:15).

Unapologetic.

"For I am not ashamed of the gospel, because it is the power of God that brings salvation to everyone who believes" **(Romans 1:16).**

In Jesus' name,

Amen.

Intention: Moving with Purpose, Not Just Motion

Let's be real. So many of us are out here doing *all the things*—calendar full, phone blowing up, every hour accounted for—and still feeling unfulfilled. Why? Because motion without purpose is just noise. Sis, being *booked and busy* means nothing if you're not aligned with what God is actually calling you to do.

That's why Esther Energy isn't about running yourself ragged trying to prove you belong. It's not about performance or perfectionism. It's about moving with strategy, discernment, and divine purpose. It's about knowing the difference between hustle and Holy Spirit-led steps.

I – Intention

Every December, like clockwork, you'll see everybody and their mama setting intentions for the new year. The goals start rolling in—more money, weight loss, new career aspirations. And listen, while all those are all good things, when we make plans and don't include God in the process, we're planning to fail. I already hear you saying, "But I do include God!" Okay, sis, the real question is: "When do you include Him?"

Is it after you've already mapped out your "master plan," and then you hit God with the "*Hey, Lord, can You bless this real quick?*" Or are you seeking Him first, asking for discipline, direction, and strategy before you even pick up a pen? Don't worry, we've all been there. I've been guilty myself—right down to the vision boards. I'll never forget hearing my favorite pastor, Darius Daniels, say, *"God won't bless who you pretend to be. He blesses who He created you to be.* "We love dreaming up big, extravagant goals, but how often do we stop and ask God, "Is this even part of Your plan for me?" When was the last time you invited Him into your process, asking where your focus should be—not just for the year ahead, but for your life? When you let God into your plans, be ready. Conviction will follow.

In 2024, I asked God to stretch my faith like never before. I didn't just write it in my journal—I lived it. I stayed consistent in prayer. I fasted, tithed, and more than anything, I started believing God for more. But here's the thing about intentionality: it doesn't just bring blessings—it initiates a deeper intimacy that invites harder conversations with God.

I'll never forget driving one day, thinking about how my sorority dues were coming up. I was trying to figure out how I was going to cover them, especially since money was tight and I didn't have steady clients at the time. Then, clear as day, I heard the Holy Spirit say: *"So you have the money for dues, but not for tithes?"* Convicted. Right there, in the car, I felt it. Not guilt or shame, but a correction you only feel when you walk close enough with God to hear Him whisper the truth you didn't want to confront.

At that moment, I realized I was giving my time, talent, and money to everything except God. I was worried about what people would think if I stepped back from my sorority, but then I heard God whisper, *"Obedience is better than sacrifice."* That was my wake-up call. It wasn't about abandoning commitments—it was about getting back into *alignment.* It was about checking my heart and asking,

> *"Are my intentions God-led... or people-pleasing?"*

> *"Am I sowing for the Kingdom or just trying to keep up appearances?"*

Alignment will put your name in rooms your feet haven't even entered yet. Just look at Mordecai.

In *Esther 6*, King Xerxes couldn't sleep. No matter what he tried, rest escaped him. But this wasn't just insomnia—this was spiritual interruption. Instead of pacing the floor or calling for entertainment, the king asked for the book of records to be read aloud to him. Of all the entries in that book, they landed on the part where Mordecai had exposed a plot to assassinate the king.

That moment wasn't random. That was God's hand at work. The king listened carefully, and then asked a simple question: *"Has anything been done to honor this man?* "The officials responded, *"Nothing has been done for him.* "Mordecai had saved the king's life and received no public recognition, no reward, no royal honor. But instead of getting bitter, he stayed in position. He didn't post about it. He didn't demand validation. He just continued walking in obedience. It didn't go unnoticed either, it just wasn't his time—yet.

When God moves, He doesn't just make room—He makes a *scene.*

The next morning, the king called in Haman, the very man who had been plotting to kill Mordecai. Thinking he was about to be honored himself by the kings question; Haman arrogantly described the kind of public celebration he believed he deserved. Robes, parades, royal attention. Then the king flipped the script: *"Excellent. Go do all of that—for Mordecai."*

The same enemy who tried to destroy him was now being used to elevate him. That's the kind of favor that can't be fabricated.

That's what happens when you stay faithful even when no one's clapping. That's what it looks like when God honors your obedience—on His terms, in His timing, and for His glory.

When you're moving with intention, there's no rush. No pressure to prove. Proverbs 14:23 reminds us, *"All hard work brings a profit, but mere talk leads only to poverty."* It's so easy to hype our plans on social media—to announce what's coming before it's even appointed. But there's something sacred about letting God do the work in you before you present it to the world.

That's when the noise fades, clarity comes, and you begin to *truly* hear from God—because you've made space for Him to lead.

So... what does it *really* look like to set Godly intention?

Let's be clear: setting Godly intentions isn't a negotiation.

It's not some spiritual quid pro quo— *"If I do this, then God will do that.* "That's not how Kingdom works.

Setting your Godly intention means humbling yourself before God—daily. It's about seeking Him in your routine, submitting your will, and allowing Him to transform you from the inside out. It is trusting him to carry what you can't.

And when you do that? Don't be shocked when the places, people, and patterns that once felt familiar suddenly feel foreign. You begin talking to God more than your girlfriends and begin to lay it all at his feet. Let me share a moment when I truly had to lay it all at His feet.

When it was time for my second oldest to go off to college, I just knew he'd stay close to home in San Antonio. But after a few talks, he started considering a school near his biological father. Now, listen... I'll keep it real. Me and his dad were cordial—but I didn't like him. I didn't like how he talked about me to our son. I didn't like how he tried to *wear* the title of "dad" but refused to *show up* as one. He wanted the recognition without the responsibility.

So, when my son told me he was thinking about moving near his dad, I felt crushed. Hurt. Rejected. I couldn't help but feel like, wow, after all I've done, you're choosing him over me?

During my morning devotion, I cried. Like, ugly cried. I wailed. I prayed. I poured my whole heart out to God. I didn't hold back either. I told God exactly how I felt. *"Lord, I know this can't be Your will. I don't understand why he would choose someone who hasn't even been consistent in his life. Why is this happening?* But in the middle of that prayer, something shifted. God softened my heart. Instead of staying in my feelings, I found myself praying, *"God, if this is Your will, protect him. Bless him. Order his steps. And Lord forgive me for all this resentment I've been carrying. Heal my heart. Change the way I see his father."*

Sis, when I tell you peace washed over me like I'd been physically wrapped up in God's arms. I knew right then and there that it was going to be okay. The very next day, I helped my son apply to every college—including the one in Dallas near his dad. I paid the application fees and just left it in God's hands. A week later, we sat down to really talk it through. I told him, "Listen, if you're going away for college, don't just bounce between parents' houses. Go all in. Live on campus. Get the full experience." We started researching dorm life, comparing schools, and weighing options.

One evening, he came running into the kitchen while I was cooking yelling, *"Mom! My acceptance letter from the University of Houston just came in! I'm gonna wait to open it with you!"* Before he told me the results, the Holy Spirit whispered, "He's going to Houston." Sure enough, he opened that letter, smiled big, and said, *"I'm in!"* I looked at him and asked, "So . . . which school are you choosing?"

With so much confidence, he said, *"University of Houston."*

Look at God. Not only did He handle the situation, but He also handled my heart in the process. That's what setting true intention with God looks like. It's laying down your personal agenda and it's releasing control. It's trusting God to work it out better than you ever could. We can be the most organized, ambitious, driven women in the room with our calendars color-coded and our goals perfectly mapped out but without God, none of it matters. He's not looking for performance, perfect words, or perfect execution. God is after you.

The introvert.
The extrovert.
The off-key singer bellowing a full concert in the car.
The daughter who's tired.
The daughter who's angry.

The daughter who's been trying to hold it together but feels like she's falling apart. All of you. Every part. Every piece.

Did you catch that I said *daughter*?

When we come to God as our Father, we talk to Him differently.

We trust differently. So today, before you plan another thing, pause. Seek Him. Set your intentions with God at the center and watch how He makes all things possible (Luke 1:37).

Prayer for Setting Godly Intentions

Father God,

Thank You for calling my name, even on the days I've been too distracted or discouraged to answer. Forgive me for the moments I've made plans without You, chasing my own ambitions instead of seeking Your will. Today, I lay it all down.

My goals.
My desires.
My plans.

Thank You for loving all of me—the tired me, the frustrated me, the joyful me, the growing me. Thank You for being intentional about meeting me exactly where I am. May every step I take be ordered by You. May every word I speak glorify You.

May every goal I set align with Your divine purpose for my

life. In Jesus' name, **Amen.**

Persistence: The Muscle Needed for Breakthrough

"Patience is a virtue, but persistence to the point of success is a blessing. "This is one of my favorite quotes because it's a powerful reminder that success isn't just about principles—it's built through consistent effort and the discipline to keep going, even when life doesn't go as planned. Truthfully, persistence is one of the hardest things we're called to as believers because it requires *radical* faith.

Not the cute, "I prayed for a parking spot, and one opened up" kind of faith. I'm talking about the gritty, deep, *"God, I'm still holding onto this promise even when everything around me says it won't happen"* kind of faith. The kind of faith that doesn't collapse under pressure—but leans in when the weight gets heavier. But don't get it twisted, persistence and faith aren't the same thing. They're different, but they work together.

Faith moves in the spiritual.
Persistence moves in the natural.
Faith gives us the courage to *start*.
Persistence makes sure we *finish*.

Persistence brings faith to life. Think of faith as the seed—believing that God's promise will grow. Persistence is the watering, the tending, the pruning, and the *waiting*. Without faith, we'd never plant anything. And without persistence, we'd walk away before ever seeing the harvest. They need each other.

Faith is what made Noah start building the ark before a single drop of rain ever fell. But persistence is what kept him hammering day after day, year after year—while the world mocked him.

Faith is what made Joseph hold onto his dreams, but persistence is what carried him through betrayal, prison, and the long waiting season—until the promise was finally fulfilled. Faith is what gave

Esther the courage to step forward, but persistence is what led her to fast, strategize, and boldly approach the king to save her people.

Faith is the why.

Persistence is the how.

P – Persistence

There are plenty of days I've wanted to throw in the towel.

But right at the moment when I felt like quitting, something inside me refuses to let go. There were even seasons when I questioned *both* my faith and my persistence. Then, I remember Jacob who wrestled with God all night long refusing to let go until he received his blessing. (Genesis 32:24–26)

Sis, what if we wrestled like *that*? What if instead of walking away at the first sign of difficulty, we pressed in, held on, and said, "*God, I'm not letting go until I see the breakthrough.* "Persistence isn't about striving in your own strength. It's about surrendering your strength to God— trusting that what *He* has for you is far greater than anything you could build or manufacture on your own.

Let's be real—it's not always easy but it's always *worth it*. It's like going to the gym. At first, the weight feels unbearable but over time, your strength increases. The same thing happens spiritually. Each time you push past discouragement, betrayal, delays, or closed doors—your spiritual endurance grows. And what once made you want to quit becomes your greatest teacher.

There are moments in life when we feel unseen, overlooked, or flat-out rejected. But what if the very thing you see as a burden is actually the place where God is birthing something powerful?

Let's take a closer look at Leah, a woman whose birthing story became one of the most powerful testaments to God's purpose and redemption. Leah was the eldest daughter of Laban and sister to the stunning and beloved Rachel. Jacob was so in love with Rachel that

131

he was willing to work seven years just to marry her. However, Leah was often overlooked, so much so that her own father had to scheme just to get her married.

Laban devised a plan for what was supposed to be Jacob and Rachel's wedding night. He got Jacob drunk and, under the cover of darkness, sent Leah in her sister's place. Unaware, Jacob slept with her, and when he finally lifted the veil, expecting Rachel—he saw Leah.

Can you imagine that? Being the backup plan in your own love story? Married to a man who didn't choose you and still longed for your sister? Leah found herself in a painful place—unwanted, unloved, unseen. But God saw her. He saw her silent tears and heard her unspoken prayers. Not only did He see her—He responded.

When God saw that Leah was not loved, He blessed her womb—while Rachel remained barren. In biblical times, children were often named based on the circumstances surrounding their birth, and we see this clearly in Leah's story—she named her sons from a place of deep brokenness.

Look at the names she gave her first three sons:

- Reuben – *"The Lord has seen my affliction."* (Genesis 29:32)
- Simeon – *"The Lord has heard that I am unloved."* (Genesis 29:33)
- Levi – *"Now my husband will become attached to me."* (Genesis 29:34)

Each name reflected her longing to be loved and seen by Jacob. With each birth, Leah's perspective slowly began to shift. She stopped waiting to be chosen by Jacob—and finally chose God instead. Then came her fourth son. She named him Judah, saying: *"Now, I will praise the Lord." (Genesis 29:35)*

Even when people don't choose you, God already has. That's the power of persistence and perspective. Sometimes, the breakthrough doesn't come from something changing around you—it comes from something shifting within you. Here's the divine plot twist: It was through *Judah*—the son birthed from surrender, not striving—that the woman who once felt unwanted was the very one God used to usher in a line of kings and, ultimately, our Savior, Jesus Christ.

So, let me ask you: How many times have you mislabeled what God is doing in your life because you we're too focused on your pain? How often do you seek validation from people who were never assigned to affirm you? All along, God is saying, *"You are already seen, loved, and chosen."*

Sis, it's time to rename that season and move forward. It's time to stop mourning what didn't happen, what didn't work out, and who didn't choose you. We've all been there—those discouraging moments when life feels stuck in place. You're just scrolling through social media, and suddenly, it feels like everyone else's life seems to be moving forward while you feel stagnant. Job promotions, marriage proposals, new babies, even follower counts—it all starts to look like a highlight reel of everything you don't have.

And before you know it, comparison creeps in and steals your joy. But hear me: your timeline is not their timeline. Your purpose isn't delayed—it's being developed. And just because it hasn't happened yet doesn't mean God's forgotten you.

After COVID, I went from being an extroverted, charismatic ball of joy to someone struggling with isolation, seclusion, and social anxiety. It was like I didn't recognize myself anymore. My husband couldn't believe it when I first mentioned it to him. Not his bubbly, life-of-the-party wife. But then, one night, I was invited out. I had already made so many excuses for why I couldn't attend other events, but this time, my husband noticed all the anxiety written all over my body language as I left the house. He didn't know I was sitting out in front of the department store, still hesitant to go in when he called.

He apologized for not recognizing it sooner. I had gotten so used to being in survival mode. For the past few years, my whole world has revolved around protecting my kids—especially my youngest.

COVID felt synonymous with death; I convinced myself that I was their only protection since my husband had been away. But here's the problem: I had placed the weight of their safety on my shoulders instead of trusting in God's protection, and that pressure was suffocating.

My husband insisted that I attend the event. "*Please push through this and go. When you come home, I promise you'll tell me how much fun you had.*" He was right, and that night, I realized something powerful—I had been mislabeling my season. I had allowed fear and anxiety to keep me stuck in survival mode long after the storm had passed.

And that's the thing about persistence—It's the difference between reaching the finish line and breaking down halfway there. If I'm being honest, I've had my fair share of "almost" moments. I would get the ball, dribble down the court, set myself up for the layup and then I wouldn't even take the shot. I struggled with follow-through.

My planners and journals are full of missed opportunities—not because I wasn't capable or smart enough, but because I let hesitation, doubt, and comparison hold me back. Then it hit me: I had been trying to do everything in the natural, when the truth is, our battles are not just physical—they are spiritual.

> *Ephesians tells us "For we wrestle not against flesh and blood, but against principalities, against powers, against the rulers of the darkness of this world, against spiritual wickedness in high places.*

I wasn't just struggling with procrastination or self-doubt—I was under attack. The enemy saw my potential before I did, and he knew that if he could stop me from moving, he could delay the assignment God placed on my life. God has given us spiritual armor, and when we suit up properly, we don't just step into battle—we step in ready to win. *"Put on the full armor of God, so that you can take your stand against the devil's schemes"* (Ephesians 6:11).

The enemy doesn't attack empty vessels. He only comes after those who are carrying something valuable—purpose, calling, anointing. If you feel like you've been fighting battle after battle, sis, that's your confirmation. God's Word never loses its power. Sis, the play has already been written, and the victory is already yours. All you have to do is take the shot.

"I'm a writer, and I'm going to publish a book. "That's what I told my husband—with full confidence—the very first time we met, fifteen years ago. Back then, my book was going to be a collection of poetry. That's who I was: the poet. The one who hosted poetry slams. The one who could take emotions and turn them into rhythm and rhyme. But that book never happened, because life did. One simple act—turning in my retirement papers—became the shift that led me to this moment.

This isn't the book I planned. This is the book God placed in me. God had already written my story—I was just catching up to the assignment.

Every trial—and there were many.
Every perceived failure.
Every detour that didn't make sense at the time.

But God was with me through it all. And here's the most humbling part: Even when I ignored the call, He never disconnected. That's what a loving Father does.

We might run.
We might resist.
We might even convince ourselves that we know better.

But just like a parent patiently waiting for their child to come home,

He's always there—arms open, heart full of grace, whispering:

"Welcome home, daughter. Now, let's get to work.

That's the kind of persistent love we have in our Heavenly Father. A love that doesn't quit or abandons but remains committed until we return home to Him. All we have to do is decrease and let God increase because perseverance is a promise and God doesn't do take backs. Sis, persist, because you're already equipped and the victory is already written. When you step into that battle, God isn't questioning whether you'll win—He's already declared that you will, you just have lean in with faith and persist to the promise.

In the military, moving up to the next rank isn't automatic—you have to pass the test. And this isn't just any test. It's 175 questions covering not only the manuals for your job but also general military knowledge. When you pass, you don't get promoted immediately—you get frocked. Being frocked means you take on the duties, wear the rank, and people address you by your new title—but the pay and benefits? Those don't come until the appointed time.

You walk in the role before you fully receive the reward.

Isn't that exactly how God works? When He elevates us, we don't always see the benefits right away. We are spiritually frocked— walking in the calling, carrying the responsibility— but the full manifestation comes in its due season. But here's where many of us fall short: We assume that one prayer, one declaration, or one act of faith is enough. This reminds me of the story of the prophet Elisha. In 2 Kings 13:17–19, Elisha instructed the king to strike the ground with arrows. The king only struck it three times and then stopped—thinking that was enough. But Elisha rebuked him, revealing that his lack of persistence cost him complete victory.

How many times do we stop short of our breakthrough? We were never meant to stop at three strikes when God was calling us to keep going until the battle was won. Just like in the military, where being frocked doesn't mean the process is over, spiritual promotion requires persistence. Esther understood this well. When Haman was executed, many would have thought the battle was over. But she knew better. The enemy had been exposed, but the decree to destroy the Jews still stood. She moved strategically, petitioning the king again.

When the king gave Mordecai his insignia, it wasn't just a symbol of victory—it was an empowerment to prepare. The Jews didn't just celebrate; they positioned themselves for the fight ahead. That's what it means to be spiritually frocked. You're already walking in the authority. You're already carrying the assignment. But to fully step into what God has prepared, you must persist, prepare, and be willing to fight until the promise is fulfilled.

Fifteen years ago, I told my husband, "I'm a writer, and I'm going to publish a book." What I didn't know then was how long the journey would be—how much waiting, preparation, and persistence it would require. God had already written my story, and it was just waiting for me to catch up to the assignment. I've learned that even in the waiting—when you feel unprepared and unrewarded—God is moving. He's healing places you didn't know were broken, growing what you can't yet see, and preparing to elevate you in His perfect timing. So here I am, at the end of this book, standing in the place I once only dreamed of. And here you are, standing at the beginning of your next level. The process doesn't stop here.

You've been spiritually frocked—set apart and appointed for such a time as this. Now it's your turn to FLIP the script on your life by walking in *faith*, *leading* boldly, moving with *intention*, and *persisting* until the promise is fulfilled. The battle may still be raging, but the **victory is yours**.

Keep striking! Your Esther Era awaits.

Sis, if you made it to this page, I need you to pause—and breathe this in:

You don't need another title to lead.
You don't need more followers to be impactful.

You don't need to wait until you feel "ready."
You are already Assigned, Anointed, and Positioned.

The world may not recognize it yet—but God already knows who you are. As you rise into your next season with Esther Energy, I want you to hold tightly to these 5 Principles—from Esther's story that are Powered by Grace and Driven by Faith:

1. Boldness – Step Forward Even When You're Scared

Esther didn't wait until she felt brave—she showed up *while afraid*. She risked her life to approach the king uninvited, knowing the cost, but trusting the call. **Boldness isn't the absence of fear; it's the decision to move anyway, knowing God goes before you.**

> **Esther 4:16** – *"If I perish, I perish."*

2. Strategy – Don't Just Move, Move with Purpose

Esther didn't rush into action—she paused, prayed, and planned. Before approaching the king, she invited her people to fast. She used discernment and timing to expose Haman's plot. **Godly strategy turns faith into focused action.**

> **Esther 5:4** – *"If it pleases the king, let the king and Haman come today to a banquet..."*

3. Obedience – Say Yes to What God Assigns

Esther didn't volunteer for the palace—God positioned her there. And when Mordecai reminded her that her role wasn't random, she obeyed. **Obedience is trusting that God knows where He's placed you and why—even when the full picture isn't clear.**

> **Esther 4:14** – *"Perhaps you have come to your royal position for such a time as this."*

4. Preparation – Be Ready Before the Door Opens

Esther didn't walk into purpose unprepared. She went through a year of refinement—both physical and spiritual. When the time came, she was ready. **Preparation is what sets you apart when opportunity calls.**

> **Esther 2:12** – *"Before a young woman's turn came to go into King Xerxes, she had to complete twelve months of beauty treatments..."*

5. Wisdom – Move in Silence When Necessary

Esther didn't expose Haman immediately. She used wisdom and discernment to gain favor first, then reveal the truth. **Wisdom teaches you when to speak, when to wait, and when to act.**

> **Esther 7:3** – *"If I have found favor with you, Your Majesty, and if it pleases you, grant me my life..."*

BONUS

6. Community – You Don't Have to Carry It Alone

Esther didn't face her assignment alone. She had Mordecai's guidance and called for the community to fast with her. **You need people who pray with you, push you, and remind you of your purpose when doubt creeps in.**

> **Esther 4:16** – *"Go, gather together all the Jews... Do not eat or drink for three days... I and my attendants will fast as you do."*

Esther Energy Prayer

Father, I come before You with a heart full of gratitude, knowing that every good thing comes from You. Just as You positioned Esther for her divine assignment, I know you have positioned me for mine—not because of my own strength or worthiness, but because of Your grace and purpose. Lord, I humble myself before You, recognizing that without You, I am nothing. My wisdom is limited, my strength runs

Esther Energy Prayer

Father, I come before You with a heart full of gratitude, knowing that every good thing comes from You. Just as You positioned Esther for her divine assignment, I know you have positioned me for mine—not because of my own strength or worthiness, but because of Your grace and purpose. Lord, I humble myself before You, recognizing that without You, I am nothing. My wisdom is limited, my strength runs out, and my plans mean nothing unless they are aligned with Yours. But through You, all things are possible.

Give me the faith to step into places I once thought was off-limits but never let me forget that it is Your hand that opens the doors. Give me the leadership to carry out the assignment with wisdom and knowledge, but keep my heart servant-minded, never seeking my own glory. Give me the intention to move strategically, knowing that every step must be guided by Your Spirit, not my own understanding. And give me the persistence to keep striking—not from pride or striving, but from a place of obedience and trust in Your perfect timing. Lord, let me be like Esther—not just bold, but humble before You. Let me always remember that favor comes from You, not man. Let me never take credit for what only You can do.

And when the breakthrough comes, when the doors open, when the victory is won—may my first response always be to bow before You in worship, giving You all the glory.

In Jesus' mighty name,

Amen

STUDY NOTES & REFERENCES

Meaning of Esther

The name *Esther* (אֶסְתֵּר) is traditionally linked to the Hebrew word "Hester" (הֶסְתֵּר), meaning "hidden" or "concealed." Though not a direct linguistic root, Jewish tradition connects this meaning to Esther's concealed identity and the unseen hand of God throughout her story.

Sources:

Abarim Publications, *Meaning of Esther* – https://www.abarim-publications.com/Meaning/Esther.html

Jewish Encyclopedia, *Hester Panim*

Esther 2:10 (NIV) – "Esther had not revealed her nationality and family background…"

Calling & Purpose

Dr. Scott Berthiaume on Christian Calling Dr. Scott Berthiaume, President of Dallas International University, reflects deeply on the Christian sense of calling: **"Three Aspects of a Christian's Calling…"**—emphasizing our call to faith, our call to service, and our call to a specific vocation—highlighting how these elements guide believers in their personal and professional journeys.https://www.diu.edu/diu-today/chapel/three-aspects-of-a-christians-calling/

The article emphasizes that *vocare* carries a deeper meaning than a job or career—it reflects an invitation into something sacred and purposeful. Source: *Seattle Pacific University – Response Magazine* *https://spu.edu/depts/uc/response/new/2012-autumn/wordplay/index.asp?*

1 John 4:4 (NIV)

"You, dear children, are from God and have overcome them, because the one who is in you is greater than the one who is in the world."

- Affirms **victory through the indwelling Spirit**.

- Reinforces the authority believers carry.

Matthew 1–14 (Overview)

- Covers Jesus' birth, baptism, calling of the disciples, miracles, and the Sermon on the Mount.

- Reveals themes of identity, divine calling, and spiritual leadership.

Luke 1 (NIV)

- Focuses on the miraculous births of John the Baptist and Jesus.

- Emphasizes Mary's obedience and surrender to God's purpose.

Proverbs 19:21 (NIV)

"Many are the plans in a person's heart, but it is the Lord's purpose that prevails."

- Encourages surrender to God's higher plans.

- Speaks directly to those discerning purpose during transition.

The following biblical stories are referenced throughout the book to illustrate purpose, identity, obedience, and calling:

David Anointed King

- 1 Samuel 16:1–13 – God sends Samuel to anoint David, the youngest son of Jesse, as king over Israel.

Leah and Rachel

- Genesis 29–30 – The story of two sisters, Leah and Rachel, their marriage to Jacob, and how God saw Leah's pain and honored her.

Jacob Wrestles with God

- Genesis 32:22–32 – Jacob wrestles with a divine being through the night and receives a new name: Israel.

The Israelites Cross the Red Sea

- Exodus 14 – God parts the Red Sea, delivering the Israelites from Pharaoh's army in a miraculous escape.

Abraham Sacrifices Isaac

- Genesis 22:1–19 – Abraham is tested by God to sacrifice his son Isaac; God provides a ram in place.

Gideon Called a Mighty Warrior

- Judges 6:11–16 – God appears to Gideon and calls him a "mighty warrior" despite his insecurities.

Hagar Runs Away

- Genesis 16 – Hagar flees into the wilderness and is met by God, who sees her and gives her a promise.

Elisha and the Three Strikes

- **2 Kings 13:14–19** – As Elisha lies on his deathbed, King Jehoash of Israel visits him. Elisha tells him to **strike the ground with arrows** as a prophetic act of victory. The king strikes only **thFree times**, and Elisha rebukes him, saying he should have struck five or six times for **complete victory**. This moment reveals how **partial obedience or limited faith can lead to limited outcomes**.

Leadership & Identity Resources

Harvard Business Review notes that "humble leadership is more than a personal virtue; it helps foster teamwork, build trust, and enhance employee well-being" — and their research shows that such leaders are not only self-aware and open to feedback, but also unlock leadership potential in others, inspiring growth, innovation, and stronger collaboration.

https://hbr.org/tip/2025/02/the-power-of-humble-leadership

Learn the 7 Distinct Leadership Styles", *Leaders.com*: Servant, Democratic, Autocratic, Transformational, Transactional, Laissez-Faire, and charismatic leadership styles are identified, each with unique strengths and challenges.hbr.org+15leaders.com+15americanexpress.com+15

Exploring 7 Common Leadership Styles: Find Your Own", *American Express Business Class*: Lists Autocratic, Pacesetting, Transformational, Coaching, Democratic, Affiliative, and Delegative styles, emphasizing that effective leaders flex between them.x.com+3americanexpress.com+3linkedin.com

6 Common Leadership Styles — and How to Decide Which to Use When" by Rebecca Knight (Apr 9, 2024)_outlines major styles like transformational, transactional, bureaucratic, laissez-faire, coercive, pacesetting, and affiliative, emphasizing choosing the right style for the context bmjleader.bmj.com+15hbr.org+15youtu

Spirit-led living

Jude 1:20-21 (NIV)

> "But you, dear friends, by building yourselves up in your most holy faith and **praying in the Holy Spirit**, keep yourselves in God's love as you wait for the mercy of our Lord Jesus Christ to bring you to eternal life."

- Being filled with the Spirit is connected to spiritual maturity and intimacy with God.

- "Praying in the Holy Spirit" implies Spirit-led prayer that aligns with God's will.

- It is an ongoing posture, not a one-time event — a way to remain grounded in faith and love.

Key Insight: The Spirit empowers believers to pray beyond their understanding and builds up their spiritual strength and endurance.

Romans 8:9, 11, 14, 26-27 (NIV)

- *"You, however, are not in the realm of the flesh but are in the realm of the Spirit, if indeed the Spirit of God lives in you." (v.9)*

- *"...the Spirit who raised Jesus from the dead is living in you..." (v.11)*

- *"For those who are led by the Spirit of God are the children of God." (v.14)*

- *"In the same way, the Spirit helps us in our weakness... the Spirit himself intercedes for us through wordless groans..." (v.26)*

Key Insight: Paul emphasizes that believers are indwelt by the Spirit — it's evidence of belonging to Christ.

- Being filled with the Spirit includes

  - Resurrection power living in you (v.11),

  - Sonship/identity as God's child (v.14),

  - Divine help in weakness (v.26),

  - Spirit-led prayer and intercession when we don't have the words.

Key Insight: The Spirit doesn't just empower but also leads, intercedes, and affirms our identity in Christ.

Media References

TODAY Show Exclusive: *"Sha'Carri Richardson speaks out about failing drug test ahead of Olympics"* – In this emotional interview, Sha'Carri shares her perspective on the pressure of performing, personal loss, and the choices that impacted her Olympic eligibility.

Accessed at:_https://www.today.com/news/today-show-exclusive-sha-carri-richardson-speaks-out-about-failing-t224363

YouTube – TODAY Segment: *"Sha'Carri Richardson regrets 'Today' show interview"* – Around the 10:40 mark, Sha'Carri reflects on how she might have approached the situation differently and the emotional toll of public judgment.

Watch at:_*https://www.youtube.com/watch?v=fAkuSIF28kY*

Prayer to Embrace Your Authority

Father God,

Thank You for choosing me, calling me, and equipping me. I am grateful for every closed door, every divine delay, and every moment You've redirected my steps, as I now see that You were preparing me for such a time as this. I surrender my doubts, my fears, and every lie that tells me I'm not enough. I am in constant need of Your guidance. Help me to walk boldly in Your authority. Remind me that it's not about being perfect; it's about being obedient. Lord, move in every part of my life so that it may glorify You. I align my intentions with Your will and ask that You continue to sharpen my discernment, strengthen my faith, and expand my territory.

Let me be a light in every room I enter. Let my work reflect Your glory. And let my legacy point back to You.

In Jesus' name,

Amen

Prayer for Strategic Preparation

Father God,

Thank You for the divine assignments You have placed on my life, even when I don't always feel qualified to carry them. Help me prepare my heart, hands, and mind for everything You have called me to. Teach me to pause and seek You first before making any decisions. Remind me that strategy without You is just busyness, but my plans are established and anointed through You. Lord, break every spirit of distraction, doubt, and comparison that tries to pull me away from what You have assigned me to do. Surround me with the right people, fill me with divine wisdom, and give me the boldness to act when the time is right. I don't want to build solely for myself—I want to build for Your Kingdom. Align my steps with Your purpose and help me walk in faith, courage, and strategic excellence, just like Esther.

In Jesus' name,

Amen

Prayer for Transformation

Father God,

Thank You for being the God of every season—the One who goes before me, walks beside me, and carries me through the unknown. In these moments of transition, when the path feels unclear and the future feels uncertain, remind me that You are doing a new thing. Open my eyes to perceive it. Open my heart to receive it. Help me to release control and surrender fully to Your perfect plan. Give me the courage to let go of what was, so I can step boldly into what is next with confidence and peace. Align my heart with Your will. Align my steps with Your purpose. Align my mind with Your truth. Like Esther, I don't want to move ahead of You, and I don't want to shrink back in fear. I want to walk in full obedience, knowing that my position, my purpose, and my promotion are all part of Your divine design. Lord, as I navigate this season, help me to trust Your timing. Strengthen my faith to believe that even in the waiting, even in the stretching, You are working all things together for my good and Your glory. I declare that I am assigned, aligned, and anointed for such a time as this.

In Jesus' name,

Amen

Prayer for Humility

Father God,

Thank You for reminding me that true leadership begins with humility. You have called me, chosen me, and set me apart for such a time as this—not to seek my own glory, but to reflect Yours. Help me to lead with grace, wisdom, and a heart that stays surrendered to You. Strip away every ounce of pride, striving, and self-promotion within me. Remind me that it is You who elevates, You who opens doors, and You who orders my steps.

When I feel unseen, ground me in the truth that I am Your special possession. When I feel the urge to control the outcome, soften my heart to trust in Your plan. When I'm tempted to push ahead without You, pull me back into alignment with Your will.

May I always remember that humility is my superpower, obedience is my strategy, and grace is my covering. As I walk this path of purpose, may my life be a reflection of Your light and love, leaving a legacy of faith, impact, and abundant blessing.

In Jesus' name,

Amen.

Prayer for Esther Energy

Father, I come before You with a heart full of gratitude, knowing that every good thing comes from You. Just as You positioned Esther for her divine assignment, I know you have positioned me for mine—not because of my own strength or worthiness, but because of Your grace and purpose. Lord, I humble myself before You, recognizing that without You, I am nothing. My wisdom is limited, my strength runs out, and my plans mean nothing unless they are aligned with Yours. But through You, all things are possible.

Give me the faith to step into places I once thought was off-limits but never let me forget that it is Your hand that opens the doors. Give me the leadership to carry out the assignment with wisdom and knowledge, but keep my heart servant-minded, never seeking my own glory. Give me the intention to move strategically, knowing that every step must be guided by Your Spirit, not my own understanding. And give me the persistence to keep striking—not from pride or striving, but from a place of obedience and trust in Your perfect timing. Lord, let me be like Esther—not just bold, but humble before You. Let me always remember that favor comes from You, not man. Let me never take credit for what only You can do.

And when the breakthrough comes, when the doors open, when the victory is won—may my first response always be to bow before You in worship, giving You all the glory.

In Jesus' mighty name,

Amen

About the Author

Reka Leftridge is a faith-based author, leadership architect, and Speaker who believes influence isn't just about being seen—it's about evoking change. A retired U.S. Navy Chief Petty Officer with over 21 years of distinguished service, Reka has served at top-tier commands, including the Pentagon, the National Security Agency, and abroad. Her leadership has shaped both military and civilian landscapes, and her voice continues to ignite transformation wherever it's heard.

As a Certified Resiliency Trainer, Navy Instructor, former Training Officer, and Director of Administration, Reka has trained and mentored leaders around the world. She now channels that same expertise into helping purpose-driven women and veteran entrepreneurs lead with clarity, confidence, and conviction. Backed by a Master's in Administration with a focus on Communication Arts and certification in Radio, Film, and Broadcasting, Reka knows exactly what it takes to command a room, build trust, and rally people around a bold vision. Whether on stage or behind the mic, her mission is simple: challenge what's possible, disrupt the status quo, and equip leaders to shape conversations that matter.

Her debut book, Esther Energy™: 5 Principles for Women of Influence, draws from her own journey through military leadership, motherhood, and faith to empower women to release perfectionism, overcome imposter syndrome, and boldly walk in their God-given assignment.

She is the founder and CEO of JCA Media & Sales, LLC, and the host of the Vet to Visionary Podcast, a content and branding agency that amplifies veteran-owned businesses and the voices that support them. She also leads MomCurateHER™, a vibrant community helping mothers curate lives of purpose and fulfillment.

Reka often jokes that she's been every kind of mom—single mom, bonus mom, and dog mom. Married for 15 years and a proud mother of four, she lives in San Antonio, Texas. When she's not behind the mic or on stage, she's mentoring future leaders, serving through Delta Sigma Theta Sorority, Inc.

Let's Connect

Ready to step into your Esther Era and go from Imposter to Unstoppable. Scan below Grab your free gift.

If you're ready to stop holding back and start confidently pursuing your God-given vision, I invite you to schedule a Clarity Call with me. We will discuss your current season, identify any obstacles you may be facing, and determine your next faith driven step. Sis, your story isn't over. God's still writing—and you get to partner with Him in curating it, with purpose and on purpose.

You don't have to have it all figured out.
You just need to say yes to what He's already placed in you.

Book your call here

www.ingramcontent.com/pod-product-compliance
Lightning Source LLC
Chambersburg PA
CBHW031530120626
46545CB00005B/2079